P9-CEO-289

Facilitating with Ease!

Core Skills for
Facilitators,
Team Leaders
and Members,
Managers,
Consultants,
and Trainers

NEW AND REVISED

Ingrid Bens, M.Ed.

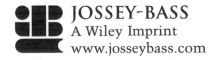

JOSSEY-BASS
A Wiley Imprint
www.josseybass.com

Copyright © 2005 by John Wiley & Sons, Inc.
Published by Jossey-Bass
An Imprint of Wiley.
989 Market Street, San Francisco, CA 94103-1741   www.josseybass.com

Except as specifically noted below, no part of this publication may be reproduced, stored in a retrieval system, or transmitted in any form or by any means, electronic, mechanical, photocopying, recording, scanning, or otherwise, except as permitted under Section 107 or 108 of the 1976 United States Copyright Act, without either the prior written permission of the Publisher, or authorization through payment of the appropriate per-copy fee to the Copyright Clearance Center, Inc., 222 Rosewood Drive, Danvers, MA 01923, phone 978-750-8400, fax 978-646-8600, or on the web at www.copyright.com. Requests to the Publisher for permission should be addressed to the Permissions Department, John Wiley & Sons, Inc., 111 River Street, Hoboken, NJ 07030, 201-748-6011, fax 201-748-6008, or e-mail: permcoordinator@wiley.com.

The materials on the accompanying CD-ROM are designed for use in a group setting and may be customized and reproduced for educational/training purposes. The reproducible pages are designated on the CD-ROM by the appearance of the following copyright notice at the foot of each page:

Facilitating with Ease! © 2005 Ingrid Bens and John Wiley & Sons, Inc.

This notice may not be changed or deleted and it must appear on all reproductions as printed.

This free permission is restricted to limited customization of the CD-ROM materials for your organization and the paper reproduction of the materials for educational/training events. It does not allow for systematic or large-scale reproduction, distribution (more than 100 copies per page, per year), transmission, electronic reproduction or inclusion in any publications offered for sale or used for commercial purposes—none of which may be done without prior written permission of the Publisher.

The material on this CD-ROM is provided "as is." neither the author of the material nor Jossey-Bass makes any warranties of any kind, express or implied, regarding either the functionality or the contents. Neither the authors nor Jossey-Bass assume any responsibility for errors or omissions or damages, including any incidental, special, or consequential damages. To the fullest extent permissible by law, Jossey-Bass disclaims all warranties of merchantability and fitness for a particular purpose.

For additional copies/bulk purchases of this book in the U.S. please contact 800-274-4434.

Jossey-Bass books and products are available through most bookstores. To contact Jossey-Bass directly call our Customer Care Department within the U.S. at 800-956-7739, outside the U.S. at 317-572-3986, fax 317-572-4002, or visit www.josseybass.com.

Jossey-Bass also publishes its books in a variety of electronic formats. Some content that appears in print may not be available in electronic books.

Library of Congress Cataloging-in-Publication Data

Bens, Ingrid.
    Facilitating with ease! : core skills for facilitators, team leaders and members, managers, consultants, and trainers / Ingrid Bens.—2nd ed.
        p. cm.
    Includes bibliographical references.
    ISBN 0-7879-7729-2 (alk. paper)
    1. Teams in the workplace. 2. Group facilitation. I. Title.
HD66.B445 2005
658.4'036—dc22   2004022750

Printed in the United States of America
SECOND EDITION
PB Printing   10 9 8 7 6

Table of Contents

Introduction

*I*t's impossible to be part of an organization today and not attend meetings. Staff meetings, project meetings, task force meetings, planning and coordinating meetings . . . the list is endless. The worst thing about many of these meetings is that they're poorly run and waste valuable time.

Over the past decade, there's been a growing recognition that effective meetings happen when proper attention has been paid to the process elements and when proceedings are skillfully facilitated.

For a long time, facilitation has been a rather vague and poorly understood practice, mastered only by human resource types. This situation needs to change. We're now spending so much time in meetings and being asked to achieve so many important goals in teams that there's a growing need for skilled facilitation throughout our organizations and our communities.

Instead of being relegated to HR, facilitation is fast becoming a core competency for anyone who's on a team, leading a task force, heading up a committee, managing a department or teaching. All of these people need to be able to create and manage effective group dynamics that foster true collaboration.

Facilitation is also a central skill for today's managers, who are riding wave after wave of change. New demands are being placed on them. At the same time, the old command and control model of supervision, which worked for decades, isn't working anymore.

To get the most from people today, leaders have to know how to create buy-in, generate participation and empower people.

To keep pace, tomorrow's leaders need to be coaches, mentors and teachers. At the core of each of these new roles is the skill of facilitation.

> *With its focus on asking instead of telling, listening and building consensus, facilitation is the essential skill for anyone working collaboratively with others.*

The Goal of This Book

This practical workbook has been created to make core facilitation tools and techniques readily available to the growing number of people who want to improve their process skills. It represents materials and ideas that have been collected, tested and refined over twenty years of active facilitation in all types of settings. This second edition retains the core tools and instruments that made the original version so popular. In addition, new materials have been added to every chapter.

As in the first edition, *Facilitating with Ease!* remains a practical workbook. While it builds on the theories of organization development pioneers such as Chris Argyris, Donald Schon, and Edgar Schein, this resource doesn't aim to be theoretical. Instead, its focus is on providing the reader with the most commonly used process tools, in a simple and accessible format. This is not so much a book to be read, as one to be used!

The Audience

This workbook contains valuable information for anyone facilitating group interactions. This is a huge constituency which includes:

- team leaders and team members
- project and task force leaders
- any supervisor or manager who holds staff meetings
- community development practitioners
- community leaders working on neighborhood projects
- teachers in traditional classroom settings
- therapists who lead support groups
- marketing consultants who run focus groups

- adult educators teaching in continuing education
- mediators of "interest-based bargaining"
- quality consultants leading process improvement initiatives like Six Sigma
- consultants intervening in conflicts
- anyone teaching others to facilitate
- anyone called on to lead a discussion or run a meeting

For the sake of clarity, many of the strategies and techniques in this book are described from the perspective of an external facilitator. These same tools work equally well, however, whether the facilitator comes from inside or outside of the group. The book also mentions team leaders and workplace teams often, but again, the tools and applications apply to any and all facilitation situations.

Content Overview

The book is organized into nine chapters. Checklists and tools have not been collected in an appendix, but are located throughout each chapter, near the related materials.

Chapter 1 outlines what facilitation is and its main applications. It differentiates process from content, and outlines the core practices. It also addresses facilitation issues such as neutrality, how assertive a facilitator can be and how to balance the role of the group leader with that of the facilitator.

Chapter 1 also describes who can best facilitate in various situations. It provides information about the language of facilitation, the principles of giving and receiving feedback, plus a thumbnail sketch of the best and worst practices of facilitators.

A new section on facilitation in the classroom has been added for teachers who use this powerful tool to enhance the education experience.

At the end of the chapter, there are two observation sheets and a four-level skills self-assessment, useful to anyone hoping for feedback on current skills.

Chapter 2 explores the stages of a planned facilitation. It describes the importance of each step in the facilitation process: assessment, design, feedback, refinement and final preparation. Helpful checklists are also provided to guide the start, middle and end of any facilitation session.

Chapter 3 focuses on knowing your participants and provides information about the four most commonly used needs-assessment techniques. Sample assessment questions and surveys are provided. This chapter also discusses the differences between facilitating groups and facilitating teams and passes along strategies for getting any group to behave more like an effective team. The creation of team norms is discussed, along with an overview of the team growth stages and the corresponding facilitation strategies that work best at each stage.

Chapter 4 begins with a frank discussion of the many reasons people are often less than enthusiastic to be involved in a meeting or workshop and provides tested strategies for overcoming these blocks, including ideas on gaining buy-in. High participation techniques are also shared, along with a training plan to encourage effective meeting behaviors in members.

Chapter 5 delves into the complexities of decision making. Facilitators are introduced to the four types of discussions and the importance of clarifying empowerment. Six different methods for reaching decisions are described and differentiated. The pros, cons and uses of each approach are explored, along with an expanded discussion of consensus building.

Chapter 5 also offers an overview of the behaviors that help decision effectiveness and provides the steps in the systematic consensus-building process. The chapter ends with a discussion of poor decisions: their symptoms, causes and cures. A survey is provided with which a group can assess its current decision-making effectiveness.

Chapter 6 deals with facilitative strategies for handling both conflict and resistance. It begins with an overview of the difference between healthy debates and dysfunctional arguments. It goes on to share techniques that encourage healthy debates and the steps in managing any conflict. Special attention is paid to facilitator strategies for venting emotions. The five conflict-management options are also explored and placed into the context of which are most appropriate for facilitators.

Chapter 6 also provides a three-part format for wording interventions that tactfully allow a facilitator to redirect inappropriate behavior. Also described are the two approaches a facilitator can choose when confronted with resistance and why one is superior. At the end of the chapter, nine common facilitator dilemmas and their solutions are presented.

Chapter 7 focuses on meeting management. There's a useful checklist and meeting effectiveness diagnostic that lets groups assess whether or not their meetings are working. There's also a chart that outlines the symptoms and cures for common meeting ills. The fundamentals of meeting management are outlined, with special emphasis on the role of the facilitator as compared to the traditional chairperson role. Both mid-point checks and exit surveys are explained, and samples are provided. Since teleconferencing is so prevalent in today's workplace, strategies are offered for using facilitation techniques during distance meetings.

Chapter 8 contains the essential process tools that are fundamental to all facilitation activities. These include: visioning, brainstorming, gap analysis, decision grids, priority setting, systematic problem solving, survey feedback, sequential questioning, force-field analysis, multi-voting, troubleshooting, needs and offers negotiation and root cause analysis. Each tool is described along with step-by-step directions for its use in groups.

Chapter 9 pulls it all together by providing ten sample process designs, complete with facilitator notes. These facilitator notes describe each meeting design in detail and set an example for how facilitators should prepare their design notes. The ten samples are the most commonly requested facilitations and provide the reader with graphic illustrations of the level of detail a facilitator needs to consider before stepping in front of any group.

After years of experience as a consultant, project manager, team leader and trainer, I'm convinced that it's impossible to build teams, consistently achieve consensus or run effective decision-making meetings without highly developed facilitation skills. The good news is that these skills can be mastered by anyone! I hope you find *Facilitating with Ease!* to be a valuable resource in your quest to gain this important skill.

January 2005   **Ingrid Bens, M.Ed.**

Questions Answered in This Book

What is facilitation? When do I use it?

What's the role of the facilitator?

What are the main tools and techniques?

What are the values and attitudes of a facilitator?

How neutral do I really need to be?

How assertive am I allowed to be?

How can facilitation be used in the classroom?

How can I facilitate when I'm not the official facilitator?

How do I get everyone to participate?

How do I overcome people's reluctance to open up?

What's the difference between a group and a team?

How can I get a group to act like a team?

What do I do if a group is very cynical?

What do I do if I encounter high resistance?

What if there's zero buy-in?

What are my options for dealing with conflict?

What if a meeting falls apart and I lose control?

What decision-making techniques are available?

Why is consensus the best method to use?

What can go wrong in making decisions?

How do I make sure that discussions achieve closure?

How can facilitation be used to manage conference calls?

How do I balance the roles of chairperson and facilitator?

What facilitation tools are available?

How do I design an effective process?

How do I know whether the meeting is going well?

What are the elements of an effective meeting design?

Some Definitions

Facilitator:
One who contributes structure and process to interactions so groups are able to function effectively and make high-quality decisions. A helper and enabler whose goal is to support others as they pursue their objectives.

Content:
The topics or subjects under discussion at any meeting. Also referred to as the task, the decisions made or the issues explored.

Process:
The structure, framework, methods and tools used in interactions. Refers to the climate or spirit established, as well as the style of the facilitator.

Intervention:
An action or set of actions that aims to improve the functioning of a group.

Plenary:
A large group session held to share the ideas developed in separate subgroups.

Norms:
A set of rules created by group members with which they mutually agree to govern themselves.

Group:
A collection of individuals who come together to share information, coordinate their efforts or achieve a task, but who mainly pursue their own individual goals and work independently.

Team:
A collection of individuals who are committed to achieving a common goal, who support each other, who fully utilize member resources and who have closely linked roles.

Process Agenda:
A detailed step-by-step description of the tools and techniques used to bring structure to conversations.

Chapter 1
Understanding Facilitation

*I*n many organizations, the idea of using a neutral third party to manage and improve meetings is now taking root. The result: the emergence of a new and important role in which the person who manages the meeting no longer participates in the discussion or tries to influence the outcome. Instead, he or she stays out of the discussion in order to focus on how the meeting is being run. Instead of offering opinions, this person provides participants with structure and tools. Instead of promoting a point of view, he or she manages participation to insure that everyone is being heard. Instead of making decisions and giving orders, he or she supports the participants in identifying *their own* goals and developing *their own* action plans.

More and more organizations are now adopting this role within their meetings. In all of the above examples, the meeting manager was acting as a *facilitator*.

What Is Facilitation?

Facilitation is a way of providing leadership without taking the reins. It's the facilitator's job to get others to assume responsibility and take the lead.

Here's an example: Your employees bring you a problem, but instead of offering them solutions, you offer them a method with which *they* can develop their own answers. You attend the meetings to guide the members through their discussions, step-by-step, encouraging them to reach their own conclusions.

Rather than being a player, a facilitator acts more like a referee. That means you watch the action, more than participate in it. You control which activities happen. You keep your finger on the pulse and know when to move on or wrap things up. Most important, you help members define and reach their goals.

What Does a Facilitator Do?

Facilitators make their contribution by:

- helping the group define its overall goal, as well as its specific objectives
- helping members assess their needs and create plans to meet them
- providing processes that help members use their time efficiently to make high-quality decisions
- guiding group discussion to keep it on track
- making accurate notes that reflect the ideas of members
- helping the group understand its own processes in order to work more effectively
- making sure that assumptions are surfaced and tested

The purpose of facilitation is enhanced group effectiveness.

A meeting without a facilitator is about as effective as a team trying to have a game without a referee.

- supporting members in assessing their current skills, as well as building new skills
- using consensus to help a group make decisions that take all members' opinions into account
- supporting members in managing their own interpersonal dynamics
- providing feedback to the group, so that they can assess their progress and make adjustments
- managing conflict using a collaborative approach
- helping the group communicate effectively
- helping the group access resources from inside and outside the group
- creating a positive environment in which members can work productively to attain group goals
- fostering leadership in others by sharing the responsibility for leading the group
- teaching and empowering others to facilitate

The bottom line goal of facilitation is group effectiveness.

What Do Facilitators Believe?

Facilitators believe that two heads are better than one, and that to do a good job, people need to be fully engaged and empowered.

All facilitators firmly believe that:
- people are intelligent, capable and want to do the right thing
- groups can make better decisions than any one person can make alone
- everyone's opinion is of equal value, regardless of rank or position
- people are more committed to the ideas and plans that they have helped to create
- participants can be trusted to assume accountability for their decisions
- groups can manage their own conflicts, behaviors and relationships if they are given the right tools and training
- the *process*, if well designed and honestly applied, can be trusted to achieve results

In contrast to the old notion of leadership, in which the leader was viewed as the most important person at the table, a facilitator puts the members first. Members decide what the goals are, make the decisions, implement action plans and hold themselves accountable for achieving results. The facilitator's contribution is to offer the right methods and tools at the right time.

Facilitating is ultimately about shifting responsibility from the leader to the members, from management to employees. By playing a *process* role, we encourage the members to take charge of the *content*.

What Are Typical Facilitator Assignments?

As a facilitator you could be asked to design and lead a wide variety of meetings. These might include:[*]

- a strategic planning session
- a session to clarify objectives and create detailed results indicators
- a priority-setting meeting
- a team-building session
- a program review/evaluation session
- a communications/liaison meeting
- a meeting to negotiate team roles and responsibilities
- a problem-solving meeting
- a meeting to share feedback and improve performance
- a focus group to gather input on a new program or product

Sample agendas for a wide range of meetings have been provided in Chapter 9.

Differentiating Between Process and Content

The two words you'll hear over and over again in facilitation are *process* (how) and *content* (what). They are the two dimensions of any interaction between people.

The *content* of any meeting is *what* is being discussed: the task at hand, the subjects being dealt with and the problems being solved. The *content* is expressed in the agenda and the words that are spoken. Because it's the verbal portion of the meeting, the content is obvious and typically consumes the attention of the members.

Process deals with *how* things are being discussed: the methods, procedures, format and tools used. The *process* also includes the style of the interaction, the group dynamics and the climate that's established. Because the *process* is silent, it's harder to pinpoint. It's the aspect of most meetings that's largely unseen and often ignored, while people are focused on the *content.*

A facilitator's job is to manage the process and leave the content to the participants.

Content	Process
What	**How**
The subjects for discussion	The methods & procedures
The task	How relations are maintained
The problems being solved	The tools being used
The decisions made	The rules or norms set
The agenda items	The group dynamics
The goals	The climate

When a meeting leader offers an opinion with the intent of influencing the outcome of discussions, she or he is acting as the "content leader."

In summary, a facilitator's job is to manage the *process* and leave *content* to the participants. When a meeting leader is neutral on the content and actively orchestrates the action, he or she is acting as the "process leader," or facilitator.

At first glance, facilitation may seem like a rather vague set of "warm and fuzzy," people-oriented beliefs. But as you'll learn, it's actually a highly structured and assertive set of practices with a rich set of tools and techniques. Once you understand these techniques and learn how to apply them, you'll immediately see substantial improvement in the overall performance of any group.

Facilitation Tools

As a facilitator you'll have an extensive set of tools at your disposal. These tools fall into two categories: *Core Practices* and *Process Tools.*

The *Core Practices,* which are rooted in the manner, style and behavior of the facilitator, include:

- staying neutral
- listening actively
- asking questions
- paraphrasing
- synthesizing ideas
- staying on track
- giving and receiving feedback
- testing assumptions
- collecting ideas
- providing summaries

The *Process Tools,* which are structured activities that provide a clear sequence of steps, include:

- Visioning
- Brainstorming
- Anonymous Brainstorming
- Force-Field Analysis
- Gap Analysis
- Multi-Voting
- Priority Setting
- Root-Cause Analysis
- Decision Grids
- Systematic Problem Solving

Understanding each of these tools and how to use them is a vital part of any facilitator's job. In Chapter Eight, you'll find detailed step-by-step instructions on how to apply these most frequently used process tools.

Core Practices Overview

Regardless of the type of meeting you're facilitating, make constant use of the following core practices:

Stay neutral on content—your job is to focus on the process elements and avoid the temptation of exerting control over the content under discussion. While you can use questions and even make suggestions to help the group, facilitators never impose their opinions or take over decision-making powers.

Listen actively—this is listening to understand more than judge. It also means using attentive body language and looking participants in the eye while they're speaking. Eye contact can also be used to acknowledge points and prompt quiet people to take part.

Facilitation has a rich set of tools and techniques.

Ask questions—this is the most important tool facilitators possess. Questions can be used to test assumptions, invite participation, gather information and probe for hidden points. Effective questioning encourages people to delve past the symptoms to get at root causes.

Paraphrase to clarify—facilitators paraphrase continuously during discussions. Paraphrasing involves repeating what people say to make sure they know they're being heard, to let others hear their points a second time and to clarify key ideas.

Synthesize ideas—ping-pong ideas around the group to build consensus and commitment. When people comment and build on each other's thoughts, it insures that the ideas recorded on the flip chart represent collective thinking.

Stay on track—set time guidelines for each discussion. Appoint a time keeper inside the group to use a timer and call out milestones. Point out digressions whenever discussion veers off topic. Park all off-topic comments and suggestions on a separate "Parking Lot" sheet, posted on a nearby wall, for issues to be dealt with later.

Use the spell-check button—since most people have difficulty spelling correctly on a flip chart, deemphasize spelling by drawing a spell-check button in the top corner of any flip sheet. Tell participants they can spell creatively, since pressing the "spell-check button" automatically eliminates errors.

Give and receive feedback—periodically "hold up a mirror" to help the group see itself so it can make corrections. Also periodically ask for feedback about the pace, process and content.

Test assumptions—facilitators always strive to bring the assumptions people are operating under out into the open and clarify them, so that they are clearly understood by everyone.

The core practices are the foundation of the facilitator's style.

Collect ideas—keep track of both emerging ideas and final decisions. Make clear and accurate summaries on a flipchart or electronic board so everyone can see the notes. Notes should be brief and concise. They must always reflect what the participants actually said, rather than your interpretation of what they said.

Summarize clearly—an effective facilitator can listen to a complex set of ideas and then offer a concise and timely summary. Summaries can also be used to revive a discussion that has ground to a halt, or to end a discussion that needs to be wrapped up. Remember that summarizing is one of the main ways to arrive at consensus.

Focus on Questioning

The importance of knowing how and when to ask great probing questions can't be stressed enough. In fact, effective questioning is *the key* facilitative technique. As a facilitator, you need to ask the right questions.

Questions invite participation. They get people thinking about issues from a different perspective. Even when acting as a neutral facilitator, you can share your good ideas by turning them into questions. Questions are also essential for getting feedback from participants about how things are going.

Facilitating is essentially a questioning activity.

Effective questioning means:

- *Asking the right questions at the right time*—select the right type of question and phrase it so that it solicits the best possible response. Then, direct it to the right person.

IF YOU WANT TO . . .	**THEN . . .**
Stimulate everyone's thinking	Direct the question to the group
Allow people to respond voluntarily or avoid putting an individual on the spot	Ask a question such as *"What experiences have any of you had with this problem?"*
Stimulate one person to think and respond	Direct the question to that individual. *"How should we handle this, Bill?"*
Tap the known resources of an "expert" in the group	Direct the question to that person. *"Mary, you have had a lot of experience in applying these regulations. What would you do in this case?"*

- *Handling answers to questions*—if a group member directly asks you for your opinion about the content, you have three options:
  1. Redirect the question to another group member or refer it to the whole group.
  2. Defer any questions that are beyond the scope of anyone present and commit to getting back to the group with an answer later.
  3. Provide the answer yourself only after signaling that you are no longer playing the process role and are now providing expert input.

Praising ideas or responding to direct questions will take you out of the facilitator role.

- *Responding to comments*—Facilitators often lose neutrality by praising an idea put forward by a member. Be careful when acknowledging the efforts of any respondents. Instead of praising the content by saying, *"That was a good idea!"* switch to praising the process instead by saying something like, *"Thank you for offering that idea."*

Question Types

There are two basic question types:

1. CLOSED ENDED
2. OPEN ENDED

Each has its uses:

TYPE OF QUESTION	DESCRIPTION	EXAMPLE
CLOSED	Requires a one-word answer Closes off discussion Usually begins with "is," "can," "how many," or "does"	*"Does everyone understand the changes we've discussed?"*
OPEN ENDED	Requires more than a "yes" or "no" answer Stimulates thinking Usually begins with "what," "how," "when" or "why"	*"What ideas do you have for explaining the changes to our customer?"*

Open ended questions are used more often and are superior to closed questions.

Questioning: Do's and Don'ts

DO	DON'T
Ask clear, concise questions covering a single issue	Ask rambling, ambiguous questions that cover multiple issues
Ask challenging questions that will stimulate thought	Ask questions that don't provide an opportunity for thought
Ask reasonable questions based on what people know	Ask questions that most people can't answer
Ask honest and relevant questions	Ask "trick" questions designed to fool them

Questioning Formats

When selecting questions to ask, there is a broad range you can choose from. It's important to understand how each of these question formats achieves a slightly different outcome.

Different types of questions create specific responses.

Fact-finding questions are targeted at verifiable data such as who, what, when, where and how much. Use them to gather information about the current situation.

  e.g. *"What kind of computer equipment are you now using?"*
  "How much training did staff receive at the start?"

Feeling-finding questions ask for subjective information that gets at the participants' opinions, feelings, values and beliefs. They help you understand views and they contain words like *think* or *feel*.

  e.g. *"How do you feel about the effectiveness of the new equipment?"*
  "Do you think the staff felt they received enough training?"

Tell-me-more questions can help you find out more about what the participants are saying. They encourage the speaker to provide more details.

  e.g. *"Tell me more." "Can you elaborate on that?"*
  "Can you be more specific?"

Best/least questions help you understand potential opportunities in the present situation. They let you test for the outer limits of participants' wants and needs.

  e.g. *"What's the best thing about receiving a new computer?"*
  "What's the worst thing about the new equipment?"

Third-party questions help uncover thoughts in an indirect manner. They're designed to help people express sensitive information.

  e.g. *"Some people find that computer training is too time consuming. How does that sound to you?"*
  "There is some concern about overly autocratic managers in many factories. Can you relate to that concern?"

"Magic wand" questions let you explore people's true desires. Also known as "crystal ball" questions, these are useful in temporarily removing obstacles from a person's mind.

  e.g. *"If time and money were no obstacle, what sort of a computer system would you design for the department?"*

Sample Probing Questions

The following sample questions are designed to delve more deeply into a problem situation.

- How would you describe the current situation in this department?
- How would your most important customer describe it?
- How would a senior manager describe it?
- How long has this situation been going on?
- What makes it worse? . . . better?
- To what extent are people aware of the problem?
- How do people feel about the situation?
- Why hasn't the problem been solved?
- Who wants change to take place? Who does not?
- Who contributes to the problem?
- How do *you* contribute to the problem?
- If the problem were totally resolved, what would the ideal situation look like?
- On a scale of 1 to 5, how serious would you say this problem is?

1	2	3	4	5
not serious at all		somewhat serious		very serious

- What are the most significant barriers to solving this problem?
- What are the parameters of this initiative? (time, money, materials)
- Are any solutions going to be taboo or unacceptable?
- How would you rate the overall level of commitment to making changes that have been agreed to?

1	2	3	4	5
Low		Medium		High

- What are some boundaries that you would suggest for this initiative?
- What would be the best possible outcome of this initiative? . . . The worst?
- What are the things that will help this initiative succeed?
- What are the potential blocks to success?
- What rules or guidelines would you like to suggest to guide the group interaction?

It's important to plan a set of questions before starting a facilitation.

The Language of Facilitation

A specific style of language has evolved as a part of facilitation. These techniques are especially important when it comes to commenting on people's behavior without sounding critical or judgmental. The main language techniques are:

- paraphrasing
- describing feelings
- reporting behavior
- perception checking

Mastering the language of facilitation will help you avoid sounding critical or judgmental.

Paraphrasing involves describing, in your own words, what another person's remarks convey.

> *"Do I understand you correctly that ..."*
> *"Are you saying ..."*
> *"What I'm hearing you say is ..."*

You should be paraphrasing continuously, especially if the discussion starts to spin in circles or if people are getting heated. This repetition assures participants that their ideas are being heard. New facilitators often make the mistake of not paraphrasing enough.

Reporting behavior consists of stating the specific, observable actions of others without making accusations or generalizations about them as people, or attributing motives to them.

> *"I'm noticing that we've only heard from three people throughout most of this discussion."*
> *"I'm noticing that several people are looking through their journals and writing."*

By describing specific behaviors, you give participants information about how their actions are being perceived. Feeding this information back to participants in a non-threatening manner opens the door for individuals to suggest actions to improve the existing situation.

Descriptions of feelings consist of specifying or identifying feelings by naming the feeling with a metaphor or a figure of speech.

> *"I feel we've run out of energy."* (naming)
> *"I feel as if we're facing a brick wall."* (metaphor)
> *"I feel like a fly on the wall."* (figure of speech)

As facilitator, you need to be in touch with how you're feeling and not be afraid to share those feelings with the group. It's very helpful to be honest with a group by telling them, *"I feel exhausted right now,"* or *"I feel frustrated."* This lets other people know that it's okay for them to express feelings.

Perception checking is describing what you perceive to be another person's inner state in order to check if you understand what he or she is feeling.

> *"You appear upset by the last comment that was made. Are you?"*
> *"You seem impatient. Are you anxious to move on to the next topic?"*

Perception checking is a very important tool. It lets you take the pulse of participants who may be experiencing emotions that get in the way of their participation.

The Rules of Wording

Since facilitators always strive to be neutral to insure that group members control outcomes, it's important to accurately record what people say without editing too much. If the facilitator changes too many words or adds words that they personally prefer, group members will feel that the facilitator has taken control of the proceedings. The first rule of recording ideas is, therefore, to faithfully record what people are saying.

Since people say much more than we can record in a few crisp statements, facilitators are always challenged to create a short, concise summary of the dialogue. This is tricky since it necessitates editing, which can lead to inadvertently changing the meaning of what is said.

Skillful facilitators are good at editing so that the shortened statement still manages to be faithful to the original idea. They do this by following these rules:

Rule #1—Use their words—Listen carefully for the key words that participants use and insure that these words are included in what gets written on the flip chart. Reinforce this by saying things like:

> *"I'm writing the word 'disaster' because you emphasized it."*

Rule #2—Ask permission to change words—If participants struggle to articulate a point or are at a loss to find the right words, offer wording, but get member approval to ensure that what's recorded reflects what people intended to say. Say something like:

> *"I've shortened what you said to this. . . . Is this OK?"*
> *"Is it okay to record that this way?"*

Another technique to keep up your sleeve is to ask people to dictate the exact words they want to see recorded. This is useful if you don't understand what they're saying or lost focus momentarily and can't remember what they said. In these situations say something like:

> *"Tell me what you want me to write down."*
> *"Give me the exact words you need to see on the page."*

This technique also works when people have rambled or shared long, convoluted ideas. Rather than taking on the task of creating a summary of their comments, ask them to take responsibility for doing this. Say something like:

> *"I want to be sure that I capture the important parts of your idea. Shorten that down to one or two crisp sentences that I can record."*

Be very careful about the words that are recorded.

Managing the Flip Chart

A flip chart may look innocent enough, but remember that these three-legged beasts can trip you, make your handwriting look like kindergarten scrawl and make even familiar spelling impossible to recall. Here are some definite *do's* and *don'ts* about flip charts.

Flip charts are essential for recording member ideas.

These dos and don'ts are as relevant to electronic recording devices as they are to paper flip charts.

DO	DON'T
Write down exactly what members say. While their comments have to be edited somewhat, always use their key words. Check to make sure that what is written captures the meaning expressed.	Write down your personal interpretation of things. These are their notes. If unsure, ask, "*What should I write down?*"
Use verbs and make phrases fairly complete. For example, writing "work group" is not as helpful as "work group to meet Monday at 10 a.m." Always be sure the flip chart can convey meaning, even to someone who was not at the meeting.	Worry about spelling. If you make a fuss, it will inhibit members from getting up and taking a turn at facilitating.
Talk and write at the same time. This is necessary in order to maintain a good pace. Practiced facilitators can write one thing and be asking the next question.	Hide behind the flip chart or talk to it. Unless you are writing, stand squarely beside it, facing the members when reading back notes.
Move around and act alive. There is nothing worse than a facilitator who acts as though he or she is chained to the flip chart. If an important point is being made, walk closer to the person who is talking so you can better pay attention.	Stand passively at the flip chart while a long discussion is going on without writing anything down. Ideas don't need to be in complete sentences before recording them. Make note of key words and ideas. Comprehensive statements can be formulated later.
Write in black, blue or some other dark color. Use fairly large letters so it can be read from the back of the room.	Use script unless you have great handwriting. Avoid red and other pale pastels that are impossible to see from any distance.
Post flip sheets around the room so that people can keep track of what has been discussed.	Monopolize the flip chart.
Whenever appropriate, let others take over both large and small group facilitation. This builds commitment and reinforces the idea that this isn't the facilitator's meeting.	Monopolize managing the meeting process.

What Does Neutral Mean?

Facilitation was created to be a neutral role played by an unbiased outsider. The role of this neutral, third party is solely to support group decision making without exerting influence over the outcome. Facilitators must, therefore, always focus on process and stay out of the content.

One of the most difficult things about learning to facilitate is staying within the neutrality boundary because facilitators often have insight into the subject under discussion. The issue of neutrality is further complicated by the fact that a lot of facilitation isn't done by disinterested outsiders, but by someone from within the group who has a real stake in the outcome.

Regardless of whether you're an outsider or a group member who has volunteered to facilitate, one of the toughest challenges is remaining neutral if you have important information that should be shared with the group or you think that the group is making a poor decision. In these scenarios, it's important to understand that neutrality can still be maintained by applying specific techniques.

1st Strategy—Ask Questions

Even though the role is dispassionate, it's important to realize that facilitators don't want to enable bad decision-making! If the facilitator has an idea that might help the group, he or she should *not* withhold it.

If the facilitator thinks that the group is overlooking an idea, the facilitator can introduce it as a question that sparks thought. For example, if the group is spinning its wheels because they can't afford new computers, the facilitator can ask: *"What are the benefits of renting new computers as an interim strategy?"*

Group members are being prompted to consider this option, but are not being told whether to accept or reject it. The facilitator's neutrality is maintained because he or she hasn't told the group what to do and decision-making control remains with the members.

2nd Strategy—Offer Suggestions

If the facilitator has a good idea that the group should consider, it's within the bounds of the neutral role to offer the group a suggestion for their consideration. He or she might say: *"I suggest that you research the pros and cons of renting computers."* Although this sounds like the facilitator has strayed into content, it's still facilitative if the content sounds like an offering, not an order. As with questioning, making suggestions doesn't violate neutrality as long as group members retain the power to decide.

Neither asking questions nor offering suggestions oversteps the boundaries of neutrality.

3rd Strategy—Take Off the Facilitator's Hat

If the group is about to make a serious mistake and all of the questioning and suggesting in the world has not worked to dissuade them, facilitators must sometimes step out of their neutral role.

In these cases, it is important to indicate that they are stepping out of the role and be clear that they are now playing a content role. He or she might say: *"I need to step out of the role of facilitator for a minute and advise you that the new computers being proposed are not within the realm of your current or future budget."*

External parties can more easily remain neutral than leaders or peers.

Since leaping in and out of the facilitator role causes confusion and distrust, taking off the neutral hat should be done very selectively. This role shift is justified when the facilitator is convinced that the group is in danger of making a major mistake. Leaders shifting in and out of the neutral role can suggest to participants that their ideas may be overturned whenever they don't match the perception of the leader.

All facilitators need to be aware that there's a difference between a neutral, external party asking a question or making a suggestion and a leader who's doing these things. When an outsider asks questions or offers a suggestion, members feel helped in their decision-making process. When their leader does the same thing, they hear an order. Therefore, staying neutral while questioning and suggesting should take into account the power relationship between the players.

How Assertive Can a Facilitator Be?

Consider this scenario. You're facilitating a meeting in which a key decision has to be made; however, two of the members get embroiled in a conflict. They take turns interrupting one another. Neither one is listening or acknowledging the other. Tempers rise. As the conflict escalates, you stand by helplessly saying nothing, in the mistaken belief that staying neutral means staying totally removed.

This scenario addresses a common misconception that taking a neutral stance on the content of meetings means being passive. This is far from the case. In fact, if you operate on the belief that your role is basically unassertive, you'll be in danger of ending up as nothing more than a note taker or scribe, while conflicts rage around you.

While it's true that facilitators should be non-directive on the topic being discussed, they have to be assertive on the process aspects of any meeting. It's within the parameters of the facilitator role to decide all aspects of the meeting process, including informing members how agenda items will be handled, which discussion tools will be used, who will speak in which order, and so on.

During discussions, a good facilitator is always assertive in managing member interactions. This involves asking people to rephrase negative comments, calling for breaks and changing the order of items if the flow needs to be adjusted.

This doesn't mean that you shouldn't collaborate with members on the session design. Gaining member input is always a good idea since it enhances buy-in. What it does mean is that process is the special expertise of the facilitator. In matters of process it's appropriate for you to have the final say.

Just how appropriate and necessary a high level of assertiveness is can be best understood when a group becomes dysfunctional. In these situations, facilitators need to be firm and act like a referee, stepping into the fray to restore order to the proceedings.

A high level of assertiveness on process is especially critical whenever there are personal attacks or other rude behavior. All facilitators are empowered to interrupt and redirect individuals so that their interactions become more appropriate. In the section on managing conflict (Chapter 6), you'll find more on techniques and language you can use for making interventions and managing stormy meetings. By following these practices, you'll be behaving in a way that's anything but passive.

Some assertive actions facilitators take, when the situation warrants it, include:

- insisting on meeting norms
- calling on quiet people
- stopping to check on the process
- calling time-outs and breaks
- intervening to stop rude behavior
- asking probing questions
- challenging assumptions
- adjusting the meeting design
- summarizing discussions
- insisting on closure
- insuring that action plans are in place
- implementing evaluation activities

New facilitators may mistakenly think they should be passive during conflicts.

Who Can Facilitate?

Once a group has recognized the need for facilitation, there's often confusion about who should take on the role. Should it be the leader of the group, a member or someone from the outside?

When to use external resources

An outsider is essential if the discussion to be held requires the full participation of all members. Choosing external facilitators to handle complex issues with large groups, such as a senior management retreat, is an excellent strategy.

External facilitators are automatically given greater credibility.

External facilitators have several advantages:
- they're assumed to be a credible, expert facilitator
- they're above the fray and can walk away afterward
- they're unencumbered by political or emotional baggage
- they can often afford to take more risks
- they don't have to live with the decisions
- they get paid for their efforts as a professional

However, being an external facilitator also offers drawbacks:
- they lack data about the group and the organization, such as its history
- they don't know the personalities of the individuals involved
- they need to create rapport and comfort to ensure trust
- they don't get to see the initiatives of the group unfold

When leaders facilitate

Leaders can facilitate most meetings provided they aren't needed as members.

Leaders have to work hard to establish their neutrality.

Leaders who facilitate have specific advantages:
- they understand the issues and resources of the group
- they know the degree of risk that can be assumed
- they feel comfortable with the members
- they know the strengths and weaknesses of individuals

The disadvantages for any leader who facilitates include:
- others may not see the leader as neutral
- the leader is not automatically given credibility as a facilitator
- the leader's presence may hinder openness
- the facilitator role may run counter to the leader's traditional style

When members facilitate

On the ideal team, all members have highly developed facilitation skills and take turns managing meetings. Like the leader, members will encounter many of the same challenges, such as having to earn credibility and working hard to stay neutral.

Members who facilitate will also have to deal with the dilemma of being cast into a leadership role, which may create a power shift within the group.

Balancing the Roles of Leader and Facilitator

When you're an outside facilitator, you'll often find yourself managing meetings at which the regular leader is also present. This can be a source of power struggles, when it needn't be.

Since there is a clear delineation between content and process functions, the two roles can easily remain distinct. Make it clear that the leader will be participating as a member of the group, while as the facilitator, you'll manage the meeting process.

Role problems often stem from the fact that the manager doesn't want to be "just a member" of the team. She or he may be used to a more controlling style and may want to dominate both the discussion and also how the meeting should be run.

All experienced facilitators have stories about clients who meddle in process designs to the point at which these designs need to be repaired mid-meeting. These repairs often represent a return to the design originally proposed by the facilitator.

Since it's the facilitator who's on the spot when a design doesn't work, leaders and members need to be diplomatically asked to give their ideas and advice, and avoid dictating the actual meeting process. This all-too-common dilemma reinforces the need to clarify roles right at the preplanning stage, so that everyone understands that the facilitator has the final say on how the meeting is run.

Many managers use external facilitators because they have difficulty staying neutral. When a manager is domineering, she or he often ends up hampering the active participation of other members.

It's quite appropriate for you to advise a potentially "controlling" manager to temper his or her role. The best way to ensure that there is close cooperation between leader and facilitator is to meet before the session and plan the agenda together. As the facilitator, you need to know what the leader wants to achieve at the session, which items are most important and how much time is appropriate for each item. There is a more detailed description of strategies for dealing with controlling leaders on page 73.

Clarify roles before the meeting to avoid power struggles.

Wearing More Than One Hat

While the rule about neutrality is beyond question, there are situations in which the facilitator may be wearing more than one hat. When this happens, it's important to tell the participants which hats are being worn and to clearly signal when you're stepping out of the neutral role.

The Expert Hat—this happens when the facilitator is also an expert in the subject being discussed. Some examples of this are a team building expert facilitating a team formation exercise or an experienced town planner facilitating a community planning discussion.

The pitfalls of being both the expert and the facilitator—unconsciously slipping in and out of the expert role so often that participants become unsure whether they're being asked to make a decision or being told what to do.

The hat balancing strategy—declare your expertise up front. Identify how the group can use your knowledge. Agree on when and how the group can access your expertise. Always signal clearly that you're switching hats before you do so. Ask someone else to facilitate those segments of the meeting where you need to join the conversation.

The Advocate Hat—this is the most difficult hat to balance with the notion of neutrality. It crops up when the facilitator has a strong set of beliefs about the topic area. Some examples are the environmentalist leading a public meeting to decide the placement of a landfill site, or the spiritual leader helping a community group to identify its goals.

The pitfalls of being both an advocate and a facilitator—structuring conversations in such a way that they point in a particular direction. Asking overly leading questions or making suggestions with such passion that participants feel pressure to agree. Slipping into unconscious selling.

The hat balancing strategy—declaring one's philosophical views at the onset so that people will be able to filter personal biases from questions. Always asking permission before expressing philosophical views and deliberately taking off the facilitator hat to add or influence content.

The Leader Hat—this is a very common facilitation combination, especially in a team environment. This occurs whenever a person with official decision-making power assumes the neutral role with people over whom they have authority. Leaders are often so used to giving opinions and making decisions that they can't relinquish control. Sometimes group members resist leaders taking on the facilitator role, either out of fear of speaking openly or because having the leader make all the decisions absolves them of responsibility.

The pitfalls of being both a leader and a facilitator—facilitating with conclusions in mind, then unconsciously driving the group to the outcome they favor. Not recognizing that followers will tend to hear their questions and suggestions as orders. Unconsciously slipping in and out of the facilitator role, which makes members distrustful of the facilitator's neutrality.

The hat balancing strategy—taking care not to declare a bias. Structuring conversations so that people are asked to look at all sides of an issue. Inviting others to challenge established ideas. Using techniques like anonymous brainstorming and multi-voting. Asking other people to facilitate discussions in which the leader bias simply cannot be put aside.

Role Dilemmas

When you lack the authority to facilitate—one of the most common role dilemmas is when the leader of the group is either unaware of facilitation or is facilitating badly, and another member wishes that they could assume the role, but feels they lack the needed authority.

The answer to this dilemma lies in the fact that facilitation is essentially a powerless role: facilitators lead by the consent of the participants. This means that anyone can become the facilitator if they ask for the role and group members agree.

This can be done on the spot in any meeting where facilitation is needed. It can also be negotiated ahead of time with the group's leader or existing facilitator. To avoid threatening others, you might identify that facilitation is your personal learning priority and ask for support from the group members while you are working to master it.

When facilitating a group of three or four people—there are lots of meetings attended by only a small group. If four people are making a decision and one of them assumes the facilitator's role, this removes a valuable resource from the conversation. Most groups can't afford to bring in an outside facilitator, nor can they afford to lose the valuable ideas of a member who plays the neutral role.

There are a number of solutions to this dilemma. The facilitator can write down his or her ideas before the meeting for presentation by one of the other group members during discussions. The facilitator can add their ideas by asking probing questions and offering suggestions. The facilitator can insure that they make their comments last after others have offered their ideas. The facilitator can also add their ideas by taking off their facilitator's hat and temporarily stepping out of the role.

Anyone can become the facilitator if participants consent.

Facilitation in the Classroom

With its emphasis on creating participation and drawing on the wisdom of participants, facilitation is a natural training tool, especially when dealing with adults. In fact, facilitation has deep roots in the practice of adult education or andragogy. You will see from the following list that the principles of how adults learn are the same as the ones that inform key facilitator strategies. These principles are that:

- adult learners are motivated to learn when they have a need
- adults learn best when they're engaged in setting their own learning goals
- adult learners are capable of self-direction
- adults possess a large bank of knowledge and learn best when they can link new skills to their existing knowledge
- adult learners have established values and attitudes that need to be considered in order to ensure that learning is relevant to them
- adults can learn by reading, listening and watching, but will learn better if they're actively involved in the process
- adult learners have a preference to relate their learning to practical applications and real world situations

A main difference between pedagogy (child education) and andragogy (adult education) is that they follow different steps:

Pedagogy	**Andragogy**
1) Present materials	1) Provide experiences
2) Memorize materials	2) Reflect on experiences
3) Practice	3) Add theory input
4) Reinforce learning	4) Identify applications

Here are some examples of facilitation activities being used in the classroom to leverage participant commitment and knowledge.

At the start of a learning activity:

- change the room arrangement from theatre style to flexible seating to allow for the creation of small groups
- acquire tools like flipcharts and markers that encourage sharing of ideas
- use interviews or a survey to assess participants' existing skills and make the class aware of the skills present in the group
- help students identify their specific learning needs
- invite participants to identify their personal learning goals and share these with the group
- link each person with a learning partner to work on assignments in a partner or team setting

Adults learn:

50% of what they see and hear

70% of what they say

90% of what they say and do.

- engage participants in conducting field research, holding interviews and gathering data about the topic
- identify case scenarios that are relevant to the learners' real-life situation
- ask participants to identify the key questions they want to have answered during the training; collect and post these

During a learning activity:

- provide case studies, class projects or other hands-on experiences to encourage participants to learn from experience
- if applicable to the subject matter, design the training to feature coaching and feedback
- structure reflection activities so that students can formulate their own theories and draw on their knowledge base
- encourage learners to formulate their own conclusions before presenting theoretical materials
- relate key learning points to back-home applications by helping participants identify implementation strategies

At the end of a learning activity:

- invite learners to write challenging questions that can be incorporated into exams
- have students take part in panels to answer questions from peers who grade their responses
- ask participants to share key learning points with their partners or project team members
- engage all participants in an evaluation of the learning process.

Facilitating in the classroom is more about supporting students as they learn, than about teaching.

In all of these activities, the educator acted as a facilitator, paying as much attention to how the learning was structured as to the content being presented. In the classroom, the facilitative trainer aims to create the conditions that support adults as they learn, rather than being primarily responsible for transmitting new information. Facilitative trainers ask questions to encourage students to seek their own answers, because adults learn more effectively using this approach. In the facilitated classroom, learners spend most of their time in exploration, discussion and feedback activities to create the learning that is most meaningful to them.

Facilitation As a Leadership Style

For decades organizations have wanted leaders to have all the answers, take charge and make the tough decisions. The result of this directive style is that many managers are "hooked" on being in control. Under these circumstances, employees are often reluctant to openly express their opinions. There are many groups that are impossible to facilitate if the official leader is in the room. After all, who's going to feel comfortable expressing an opinion if there's even the slightest chance it might contradict what the "boss" thinks? An employee who feels this way will tell you that he or she doesn't want to make decisions and isn't paid enough to be held accountable.

Today's managers are using facilitation as a cornerstone of their leadership style.

Over the decades, the "command and control" model of leadership has created a culture in which those at the front line have been relegated to the role of "doers" and totally underutilized as thinkers. This directive leadership style is in decline today. This style may have worked in the old-fashioned world of assembly lines, but it's a terrible waste of human resources in today's knowledge-driven world.

Today's organizations need to harness the intelligence, commitment and energy of all their members. This level of engagement can only be fostered by a shift in leadership: from telling to asking, from controlling to facilitating. While there's a pressing need for all leaders to become more facilitative, this is often a difficult challenge.

The transition to facilitative leadership is hampered by the old notion that those in a leadership position ought to make most final decisions. The fastest way any leader can change his or her directive style is to become facilitative at meetings. Instead of participating in the discussion, leaders can use facilitation to empower and ensure that other people's best ideas are brought out. Of course, this is easier said than done.

Using facilitation means learning to live with the decisions of others.

The reality is that facilitation promotes a more democratic way of making decisions, which is a major adjustment for some leaders. While there will always be some decisions that should be made by one person, a facilitative leader aims to create consensus on issues. Managers who adopt facilitation, therefore, need to accept that consensus and majority voting will become the dominant decision-making methods. Shifting one's style to facilitation means learning to live with the decisions of others.

Some managers try to get the best of both worlds by having one of their team members become an expert at facilitation, while they stay in the control mode. While this may seem to work, the leader will ultimately discover that using facilitation makes the group's culture more democratic regardless of who is actually standing at the flip chart.

Managers who are reluctant to facilitate sometimes fear they'll be left with no real role to play. This is a misconception. When a leader facilitates, he or she is needed just as much as before because "process" leadership is such a full and important job.

The Power of Facilitation

When leaders shift their paradigm from controlling and directing to facilitating and empowering, they often feel as though they've given up all of their familiar "power tools." In reality, there's a substantial amount of power and control built into the role of facilitator. The difference is that this power is exerted indirectly—through the application of process, rather than through control of content. Consider the following examples of how process can be used to manage and control the activities of a group.

Situation	Old Directive Approach	Facilitative Process Approach
Members misbehave	↪ give them a pep talk about getting along	↪ have members create rules they agree to abide by
A bad decision is made	↪ overturn it, then explain why	↪ have members critique their decision using objective criteria
Members overstep their authority	↪ rein them in, supervise more carefully	↪ expand empowerment to meet the needs of specific situations

When operating in a group setting, a facilitator actually has much more control than a manager operating without process tools. With process knowledge, a leader can exert tremendous influence. Using a facilitative process approach, leaders can:

- get groups to set and commit to ambitious goals
- build and maintain high-performance teams
- run efficient and highly effective meetings
- engage groups in process improvement
- settle conflicts between groups
- systematically solve organizational problems
- manage interpersonal dynamics

Rather than viewing facilitation as a disempowering change, leaders need to see the inherent advantages in being a "master of process."

Facilitation techniques give leaders tools for managing groups.

The Impact of Facilitating

Never underestimate how a shift in leadership paradigm impacts others. When you're a leader who facilitates, staff are encourged to stop relying on you for answers and will draw on their own resources. Instead of coming to you with questions, they learn to bring solutions. Instead of complying with orders, they'll participate in creating plans to which they'll have a high level of commitment. When presented with more information, they'll offer more ideas. When given more decision-making authority, they'll weigh options more carefully. Instead of waiting for direction, they'll become engaged in setting the direction.

When you adopt a facilitative approach, each group member becomes a leader because there are opportunities to take initiative. In fact, the hallmark of a good leader is that all of the group's members become leaders themselves. Similarly, the sign of a great facilitator is that all members of the group become skilled facilitators, too.

Facilitation skills are central to other important leadership functions.

Facilitation As a Core Leadership Competency

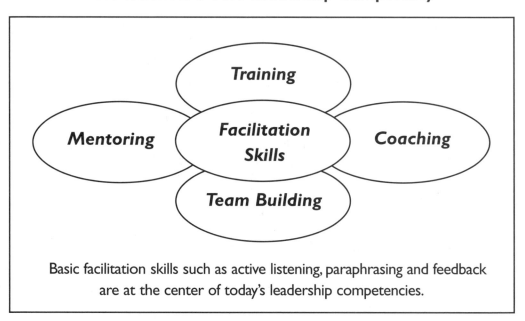

Basic facilitation skills such as active listening, paraphrasing and feedback are at the center of today's leadership competencies.

Best and Worst Facilitator Practices

Some of the best things that a facilitator can do:

→ carefully assess the needs of the members
→ probe sensitively into people's feelings
→ create an open and trusting atmosphere
→ help people understand why they're there
→ view yourself as serving the group's needs
→ make members the center of attention
→ speak in simple and direct language
→ work hard to stay neutral
→ display energy and appropriate levels of assertiveness
→ champion ideas you don't personally favor
→ treat all participants as equals
→ stay flexible and ready to change direction if necessary
→ listen intently to fully understand what's being said
→ make notes that reflect what participants mean
→ periodically summarize related ideas into a coherent summary
→ know how to use a wide range of process tools
→ make sure every session ends with clear steps for the next meeting
→ insure that participants feel ownership for what has been achieved
→ end on a positive and optimistic note

Some of the worst things a facilitator can do:

→ remain oblivious to what the group thinks or needs
→ never check member concerns
→ fail to listen carefully to what's being said
→ lose track of key ideas
→ take poor notes or change the meaning of what's said
→ try to be the center of attention
→ get defensive
→ get into personality battles
→ put people down
→ avoid or ignore conflict
→ let a few people or the leader dominate
→ never check how the meeting is going
→ be overly passive on process
→ push ahead on an irrelevant agenda
→ have no alternative approaches
→ let discussions get badly sidetracked
→ let discussions ramble without proper closure
→ be oblivious about when to stop
→ be insensitive to cultural diversity issues
→ use inappropriate humor

Facilitator Behaviors and Strategies

Regardless of whether you're a facilitator from within the group or from outside, the team's leader or a member, the following are parameters for facilitator behaviors.

Be Informed—Successful facilitators always gather extensive data about their prospective participants in order to fully understand both their business and their needs. They survey and interview participants, read background reports and use prepared questions to build a complete picture of the group's situation.

Be Optimistic—Facilitators don't let disinterest, antagonism, shyness, cynicism or other negative reactions throw them off. Instead, they focus on what can be achieved and strategies to draw the best from each participant.

Be Consensual—Facilitation is fundamentally a consensus-building process. Facilitators always strive to create outcomes that reflect the ideas of all participants equally.

Be Flexible—Successful facilitators always have a process plan for all meetings, yet at the same time are always ready to toss it aside and change direction if that's what is needed. Really great facilitators possess a wide repertoire of process tools and come prepared with alternative strategies.

Be Understanding—Facilitators need to understand that there are great pressures on employees in today's workplace and that antagonistic or cynical behaviors may be a result of high stress levels.

Be Alert—Accomplished facilitators are expert people watchers. They pay careful attention to group dynamics and notice what's going on at all times. They are attuned to noticing both how people interact and how well they're achieving the task.

Be Firm—Good facilitation is not a passive activity, but one that calls for substantial assertiveness. Facilitators should always be ready to step in and redirect an ineffective process.

Be Unobtrusive—The facilitator should do as little talking as possible. The participants should be doing all of the talking. The facilitator says only enough to give instructions, stop arguments, keep things on track and sum up. Trying to be the center of attention or make yourself look important is a misuse of your position.

> *Facilitating should be an egoless activity. The purpose is to make the group succeed, not to make you look really important and clever. An effective facilitator will leave a group convinced that "We did it ourselves!"*

Facilitation Cue Card

To start a facilitation

- welcome participants
- introduce members
- explain your role
- clarify session goal
- ratify agenda
- explain the process
- set time frames
- appoint time keeper
  and minute taker
- start the discussion

Remember to:

- stay neutral
- make eye contact
- include quiet people
- ask probing questions
- weave ideas together
- paraphrase actively
- park off-topic items
- refer questions to members

During a facilitation

- check the purpose
  for clarity
- check the process
  for effectiveness
- check the pace:
  ...Too fast? ...
  Too slow?
- take members' pulse
- summarize periodically
  and at end of session

Manage conflict by:

1. *Venting feelings:*
   - listen
   - empathize
   - clarify
2. *Resolving the issue:*
   take a problem-solving
   approach and end with clear
   action steps

To end a facilitation

- help members make a
  clear statement of
  what was decided
- develop clear next steps
  with dates and names
- round up leftover items
- help create next agenda
- clarify follow-up process
- evaluate the session

Tool kit

Visioning
Sequential Questioning
Brainstorming
Force-Field Analysis
Multi-Voting
Root Cause Analysis
Decision Grids
Troubleshooting
Systematic Problem-Solving

Be Soft on People—Hard on Issues!

Learning to facilitate takes practice.

Practice Feedback Sheets

An excellent way of improving your facilitation skills is to ask a colleague to observe you in action and give you feedback. On the following pages are two different observation sheets for feedback purposes. The first focuses on core practices, while the second emphasizes the key elements in an effective process.

Regardless of which sheet is used, the following steps are suggested:

1. First describe what you think you did well. Ask yourself: *"What did I do effectively? What were my strengths?*

2. Next, invite the observer to offer their specific observations of the things that they saw you do well.

3. Finally, have the observer provide concrete suggestions for improvements that would enhance your facilitation effectiveness.

✎ Notes

_____

_____

_____

_____

_____

_____

_____

_____

_____

_____

_____

_____

_____

Core Practices Observation Sheet

 Facilitator:

Behaviors that help

___ listens actively

___ maintains eye contact

___ helps identify needs

___ gets buy-in

___ surfaces concerns

___ defines problems

___ brings everyone into the discussion

___ uses good body language and intonation

___ paraphrases continuously

___ accepts and uses feedback

___ checks time and pace

___ provides useful feedback

___ monitors and adjusts the process

___ asks relevant, probing questions

___ keeps an open attitude

___ stays neutral

___ offers helpful suggestions

___ is optimistic and positive

___ manages conflict well

___ takes a problem-solving approach

___ stays focused on process

___ ping-pongs ideas around

___ makes accurate notes that reflect the discussion

___ effectively uses humor

___ looks calm and pleasant

___ is flexible about changing the approach used

___ skillfully summarizes what is said

___ knows when to stop

Behaviors that hinder

___ is oblivious to group needs

___ no follow-up on concerns

___ poor listening

___ strays into content

___ loses track of key ideas

___ makes poor notes

___ ignores conflicts

___ provides no alternatives for structuring the discussion

___ gets defensive

___ doesn't paraphrase enough

___ lets a few people dominate

___ never checks how it's going

___ is the center of attention

___ lets the group get sidetracked

___ projects a poor image

___ uses negative or sarcastic tone

___ talks too much

___ puts people down

___ doesn't know when to stop

Additional Observations:

Process Flow Observation Sheet

 Facilitator:

Clarifies the purpose

Creates buy-in if needed

Checks assumptions

Makes sure there are norms

Establishes the process

Sets time frames

Stays neutral and objective

Paraphrases continuously

Acts lively and positively

Makes clear notes

Asks good probing questions

Makes helpful suggestions

Encourages participation

Addresses conflict

Sets a good pace

Checks the process

Moves smoothly to new topics

Makes clear and timely summaries

Knows when to stop

Facilitation Skill Levels

Mastering the art of neutrality, keeping notes and asking questions at meetings is not all there is to facilitating. Being a true facilitator means developing your competency at four distinct levels.

Review the skills needed at each of the four levels described below. Then complete the facilitation skills and needs assessment instrument that follows to identify your current strengths and future training needs.

Level 1

Understanding concepts, values and beliefs; use of facilitative behaviors such as active listening, paraphrasing, questioning, summarizing; managing time; encouraging participation; keeping clear and accurate notes; using basic tools like problem solving and action planning.

Level 2

Mastering process tools; designing meetings; skilled at using the right decision-making method, achieving consensus and getting true closure; handling feedback activities and conducting process checks; using exit surveys; good at managing meetings in an effective manner; able to help a group set goals and objectives that are measurable; skilled at checking assumptions and challenging ideas.

Level 3

Skilled at managing conflict and making immediate interventions; able to deal with resistance and personal attacks; making design changes on the spot; sizing up a group and using the right strategies for its developmental stage; managing survey feedback exercises; able to design and conduct interviews and focus groups; design and implement surveys; consolidating ideas from a mass of information into coherent summaries.

Level 4

Design and implement process interventions in response to complex organizational issues; use tools to promote process improvement, customer intimacy and overall organizational effectiveness; able to support teams in the various stages of team development.

Facilitation Skills Self-Assessment

Assess your *current* skill levels by rating yourself according to the basic skill areas outlined below.

Rank your *current* skill level using the five-point scale below.

1	2	3	4	5
skills lacking		some skills		total mastery

Level 1   Rating

1. Understand the concepts, values and beliefs of facilitation _____

2. Skilled at active listening, paraphrasing, questioning and summarizing key points _____

3. Able to manage time and maintain a good pace _____

4. Armed with techniques for getting active participation and generating ideas _____

5. Keep clear and accurate notes that reflect what participants have said _____

6. Familiar with the basic tools of systematic problem solving, brainstorming and force-field analysis _____

Level 2

1. Knowledge of a wide range of procedural tools essential for structuring group discussions _____

2. Able to design meetings using a broad set of process tools _____

3. Knowledge of the six main decision-making approaches _____

4. Skilled at achieving consensus and gaining closure _____

5. Skilled at using feedback processes. Able to hear and accept personal feedback _____

6. Able to set goals and objectives that are measurable _____

7. Able to ask good probing questions that challenge own and others' assumptions in a non-threatening way _____

8. Able to stop the action and check on how things are going _____

9. Able to use exit surveys to improve performance _____

10. Able to manage meetings in an orderly and effective manner _____

Level 3

1. Able to manage conflict between participants and remain composed _____

2. Able to make quick and effective interventions _____

3. Able to deal with resistance non-defensively _____

4. Skilled at dealing with personal attacks _____

5. Able to redesign meeting processes on the spot _____
6. Able to size up a group and use the right strategies for their _____
   developmental stage
7. Able to implement survey feedback exercises _____
8. Able to design and conduct interviews and focus groups _____
9. Knowledgeable about survey design and questionnaire _____
   development
10. Able to integrate and consolidate ideas from a mass of _____
    information and create coherent summaries

Level 4

1. Able to design and implement process interventions in _____
   response to complex organizational issues
2. Able to facilitate process improvement, customer intimacy _____
   and other organization development activities
3. Able to support teams in their forming, storming and _____
   performing stages

My current skills (Include all the items you ranked as 4 or 5)

_____

_____

_____

_____

The skills I most need to work on (Choose the ones most immediately
important from all the ones ranked as 1 or 2)

_____

_____

_____

_____

_____

✎ Notes

Chapter 2
Facilitation Stages

*O*ne of the biggest mistakes you can make as a facilitator is to come to a meeting without having assessed the situation or prepared design notes for the session. Before you facilitate any meeting, you should be aware of the specific stages involved to insure proper planning and implementation.

While the following steps are most often followed by an external facilitator, these steps can also be used if you're an internal person who's asked to plan and run a complex meeting or workshop.

Stages in Conducting a Facilitation
1. Assessment and Design
2. Feedback and Refinement
3. Final Preparation
4. Starting a Facilitation
5. During a Facilitation
6. Ending a Facilitation
7. Following Up on a Facilitation

Preparation is as important as the facilitation itself.

1. Assessment and Design

The first step in ensuring success in any facilitation is to make sure the meeting design is based on sufficient and adequate information.

If you're coming from outside, ask the group's leader to send a letter to all members, informing them that an external facilitator has been brought in and that you will be contacting them to gather background information.

The best way to start is to interview the person who asked you to facilitate the meeting. In addition to this person, it's important to also gather information from other members. Always check your and their assumptions by gathering data from a cross-section of members. There's nothing worse than basing the design of a meeting on what the leader has told you, only to find that no one else in the group agrees with that assessment. Think of all that wasted time, plus the pressure of adjusting a meeting design on-the-spot.

To assess the needs and status of the group, you can use one or more of the following techniques:

- one-on-one interviews
- surveys
- group interviews
- direct observation

Samples and details of each technique are included in Chapter 3, starting on page 49.

Any time you gather data about a group, a summary of that information *must* always be fed back to the members. This can be done by providing the members with a written summary of the assessment notes or by writing key points on a flip chart and reviewing them briefly at the start of the session.

If possible, share this feedback before the meeting agenda is presented. If you've done a good job, the design of the meeting should sound like it flows directly from the information gathered.

Insure that the members understand and ratify the meeting design.

Once all the data is in and you feel confident that you understand the group and their needs, you can create a preliminary design. This includes identifying the objectives of the session and writing an agenda with detailed process notes. Refer to page 185 for examples of process notes.

2. Feedback and Refinement

Once you've created a proposed agenda for the session, it's wise to share that design with group members to get their input and approval.

If your design is intended for a large group or a complex event, like a planning retreat, this feedback activity will need to be more formal. It's common to meet with a representative sub-group of members so that they can hear the feedback from the data gathering and review the proposed design being presented. If the design is for a smaller, less complex meeting, it may suffice to discuss your agenda ideas with the leader and/or representative member.

There are many situations in which the group's members may not like what you've designed. There's often a gap between what a group wants and what the facilitator thinks they need.

Don't back down too easily if you feel the group really needs to discuss certain items.

If a disagreement about the design arises, you need to insure that all viewpoints are heard and that optional designs are considered. If the group has valid reasons for not wanting to do an exercise (i.e., the content is too sensitive to discuss, the objectives have changed, etc.), respect that concern.

On the other hand, you should stand firm and assertively promote your design, especially if meeting members are new or reluctant to use participatory techniques or have a history of dysfunction. In these cases, listen to their objections, then help them understand your recommendations. Sometimes what they want is not what they need.

Once agreement on a final workshop design has been reached, you can write a brief summary of both the feedback and final version of the design and send it to the group's representatives. This written memo will help reduce the potential for misunderstanding.

3. Final Preparation

Professional facilitators spend as much time preparing for a facilitation session as they do leading the actual event. The industry standard for session leaders is one day of preparation for each day of facilitation. Some complex sessions even have a ratio of two days of preparation for each day of facilitation.

Here are common time allocations for facilitation assignments:

Workshop/ Meeting Length	Interview Time	Design Time		Total Time
1–day workshop (18 people)	1/2 day	1/2 day	➡	2 days
2–day workshop (18 people)	1 day	1 day	➡	4 days
2–day retreat (60 people)	1 day	3 days	➡	6 days

Facilitators spend as much time planning as they spend in front of groups.

What should be done as part of the final preparation:

 __ finalize the design and put it in writing for the client

__ clarify the roles and responsibilities of all parties

__ check the suitability of the meeting location

__ help the group leader prepare a letter detailing meeting logistics and the final agenda for distribution

__ identify all needed materials and supplies required

__ design and write all workshop materials and handouts

__ complete all handouts and required flip charts

The members of the group are typically responsible for sending notices, arranging and paying for logistics such as accommodations, insuring that a suitable meeting room is available, arranging and paying for printing, keeping clear minutes of the proceedings, transcribing all flip chart notes, monitoring to insure follow-through on all action plans and evaluating the results.

4. Starting a Facilitation

As the facilitator, you should always be the first person to arrive for any meeting. This insures that there's time to make last-minute seating changes in the meeting room, post the agenda and survey data, test the equipment and so on.

Room set-up is critical for sessions. A large room with modular furniture works best for both large group and subgroup settings. Huge boardroom tables, on the other hand, are detrimental to creating an atmosphere conducive to dialogue. A long table also tends to reinforce hierarchical patterns and discourage eye contact between members.

When facilitating large groups it's best to seat attendees at round tables spaced evenly around the room. Small table groups consisting of between five to eight persons are ideal.

Make sure there is ample wall space for posting the flip chart notes that will be generated throughout the day. Lots of easels are usually needed; order one for each subgroup and two for the front of the room.

Chatting informally with members as they arrive not only helps break the ice, it gives people an opportunity to get to know you.

Over time you'll develop your own personal approach for beginning a session; here's a check list to get you get started:

___ introduce yourself and give a brief personal background

___ clarify the role you'll be playing as the facilitator

___ clarify the roles to be played by any other members

___ go around the room and have members introduce themselves by name and perhaps position, especially if there are people present who don't know each other

___ conduct a warm-up activity to relax the group; make sure this fits with the time available and activity focus

___ review any data collected from members; have key points written on flip chart paper, on overheads or PowerPoint; answer questions about the data

___ clarify the goal and the specific objectives of the session

___ review the agenda and invite comments; make any needed changes to assure acceptance of the agenda

___ specify time frames; appoint a timekeeper

___ take care of all housekeeping items

___ help the group set norms for the session; post these on a wall within clear view of all members; if norms exist, review them and ask for additions

___ set up a parking lot sheet on a side wall to keep track of digressions

___ proceed to the first item on the agenda; make sure everyone's clear about the purpose of the first discussion

___ explain the process, or how you'll be handling this agenda item

___ be sure that the time frame for the first item is set

___ get on with the discussion

Be the first to arrive and pay attention to room set-up.

Start each discussion by specifying:
* *Purpose,*
* *Process,*
* *Time.*

5. During a Facilitation

Your key contribution during any meeting is to provide the structure and process focus that will keep the discussion moving efficiently and effectively.

You'll need to:

__ insure that all members participate

__ manage any conflicts or differences of opinion

__ keep the group on topic and park off-topic items

__ monitor time and maintain an appropriate pace

__ help members adhere to their ground rules

__ make interventions if there are problems

__ maintain a high energy level and positive tone

__ help members articulate key points

__ keep track of ideas by making concise notes

During any meeting, periodically employ the following process checks:

Constantly monitor how the discussion is going.

Check the purpose—periodically check to see that everyone is still clear about the focus of the conversation by asking:

"Is everyone still clear about what's being discussed?"

"Are we still discussing our topic or have we shifted our focus?"

Restate the purpose of the discussion to refocus members.

Check the process—periodically ask members if the approach being used is working, by asking:

"We said we would work this issue through as a large group, rather than sub-grouping. Is this approach working or should we try something else?"

Adjust the process throughout the session to insure that things keep working.

Check the time—ask members how the pace feels to them by asking:

"Is this session dragging or are you feeling rushed?"

"What can we do to improve the pace?"

Respond to their assessments by implementing needed adjustments.

Take the pulse of members—continuously read faces and body language to determine how people are feeling. Don't hesitate to ask:

"How are members feeling?"

"Is anyone feeling like they've dropped out?"

"How can we get our energy levels up again?"

Reading people lets you know when to stop for a break or bring lost members back into the fold.

Use process checks to stay on track.

6. Ending a Facilitation

A common problem in many meetings is lack of closure. Lots of things get discussed, but there's no clear path forward. One of your key contributions is to insure that decisions are reached and detailed action steps are in place before moving to the next topic or adjourning the meeting.

Here are some ways you can help a group bring effective closure to a meeting:

Discussions that end without closure waste everyone's time!

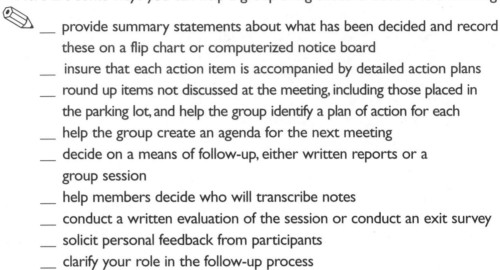

___ provide summary statements about what has been decided and record these on a flip chart or computerized notice board

___ insure that each action item is accompanied by detailed action plans

___ round up items not discussed at the meeting, including those placed in the parking lot, and help the group identify a plan of action for each

___ help the group create an agenda for the next meeting

___ decide on a means of follow-up, either written reports or a group session

___ help members decide who will transcribe notes

___ conduct a written evaluation of the session or conduct an exit survey

___ solicit personal feedback from participants

___ clarify your role in the follow-up process

Close by thanking participants for the opportunity to facilitate.

7. Following Up on a Facilitation

No matter how formal or informal the facilitation process has been, following up with the group is always a good idea. If the facilitation consisted of a brief meeting, you might simply call the group leader to determine the extent to which the session helped the group become more effective. If the session was a major decision-making workshop or retreat, encourage the group leader to send out a written follow-up questionnaire to the members.

Unless it was formally agreed that you would conduct the follow-up activity, you can leave any post-session reports to the group's members. This insures that they, not you, assume accountability for the implementation of the ideas emerging from the session. Your role may be to merely remind the group about the need for follow-up and to provide them with a format for reporting results later.

In some cases, you may negotiate with the group to facilitate a follow-up meeting at which the progress is discussed and evaluated.

Follow-Up Report Format

Please provide your feedback and update information about our session.

Date:_____

Objective(s) of the meeting:_____

Results achieved: What were the major outcomes of the meeting?

Work completed: Which action plans created at the session have been completed? What was achieved?

Work outstanding: Which action items are still in progress or in the planning stages? What are the time frames for these activities?

Next steps: Are there any next steps that need to be planned by the whole group?

Use a follow-up report format to encourage follow-through.

✎ Notes

Chapter 3
Knowing Your Participants

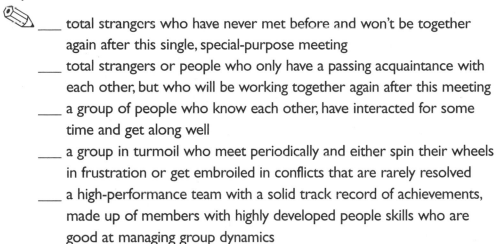

Getting to know the people you'll be working with is an essential first step in designing any effective meeting. Before you facilitate, you need to know if they are:

_____ total strangers who have never met before and won't be together again after this single, special-purpose meeting

_____ total strangers or people who only have a passing acquaintance with each other, but who will be working together again after this meeting

_____ a group of people who know each other, have interacted for some time and get along well

_____ a group in turmoil who meet periodically and either spin their wheels in frustration or get embroiled in conflicts that are rarely resolved

_____ a high-performance team with a solid track record of achievements, made up of members with highly developed people skills who are good at managing group dynamics

Always take the time to get to know your participants.

Conducting an Assessment

Never take a group or situation for granted. Different situations require distinct activities. It's up to you to carefully read a group and design a process that matches their circumstances. So, how do you get the information you need? Try one of these approaches:

- **One-on-one interviews** allow you to question people about the state of the team and member interactions. This is the best way to get people to open up and be candid when there are sensitive issues in the group.

- **Group interviews or focus groups** are a good strategy when the subject isn't overly sensitive and/or there are too many people to interview singly. Group interviews let you observe the group dynamics before the actual facilitation session.

- **Surveys** let you gather anonymous information from all members. They enable you to compile answers to the same questions from each member. They also generate quantifiable data.

- **Observing the group in action** helps you understand the interpersonal dynamics. This involves sitting on the sidelines during meetings in order to get a sense of who plays which roles and how people relate to each other. It's very useful if the team is in conflict.

Assessment Questions

When meeting a new group, you'll need to ask certain questions to determine the state of the group. Here are some questions that may be useful:

- What's the history of the group?

- How familiar are members with each other?

- Are there clear goals?

- Are there team norms or rules?

- Does everyone participate or do a few dominate?

- To what extent are members honest and open?

- Do members listen to and support each other's ideas?

- How does the group handle any conflicts?

- How are important decisions made?

- Do people usually leave meetings feeling like something has been achieved?

- How would you describe the group atmosphere?

- Are meetings thoroughly planned and structured or are they basically freewheeling?

- Does the group ever stop to evaluate how it's doing and make corrections?

- What's the best thing about the group? What's the worst?

- How do people feel about being part of this group?

- Describe a recent incident that illustrates how members typically interact.

- Are there any reasons why members might not be open and say what they really think?

- Why do you need (external) facilitation support? Is there any opposition to this?

- What's the worst thing that could happen at this meeting? What could be done to insure that this doesn't happen?

These questions are presented in survey form on the next page.

Group Assessment Survey

1. How familiar are members of this group with each other?

1	2	3	4	5
Passing acquaintances		Some of us know each other		We are a high-performance team

2. Are there clear goals for the group?

1	2	3	4	5
We have no stated goals		Not sure about the goals		We have clear goals

3. Does the group have a clear set of rules to manage interactions?

1	2	3	4	5
No rules exist		There are norms that we created		We have and use rules but they aren't used effectively

4. Describe the typical participation pattern.

1	2	3	4	5
A few people dominate		Participation varies from topic to topic		We have and use rules but they aren't used effectively

5. How much honesty and openness is there in this group?

1	2	3	4	5
People hide what they really think		We are somewhat open		We are totally open and honest

6. How good are members at listening, supporting and encouraging each other?

1	2	3	4	5
We don't do this at all		We try but don't always succeed		We are consistently excellent

7. How do members typically handle differences of opinion?

1	2	3	4	5
We get emotional and often argue		It varies		We always debate objectively and respectfully

Group Assessment Survey, cont'd

8. How are important decisions usually made?

1	2	3	4	5
We often resort to voting		Our approach varies		We strive for consensus

9. Does the group usually end its meetings with a sense of achievement and clear action plans?

1	2	3	4	5
Never		Sometimes		Always

10. How would you describe the atmosphere between members?

1	2	3	4	5
Hostile and tense		Satisfactory		Totally relaxed and harmonious

11. How would you describe the group's meetings?

1	2	3	4	5
Unstructured: waste of time		Satisfactory		Well planned and productive

12. Does the group ever stop and evaluate how it's doing and then take action to improve?

1	2	3	4	5
Never		Sporadically		Consistently

Note: See page 170 for instructions on conducting a survey feedback exercise.

Comparing Groups to Teams

In order to design appropriate meeting processes, it's important for you to be aware of the differences between groups and teams, as well as the significant differences between teams at the forming, storming, norming and performing stages of their development.

What Is a Group?

A group is a collection of people who come together to communicate, tackle a problem or coordinate an event. Even though they may meet often, they're a group and not a team because they have specific traits. In most groups:

- individual members operate under their own separate parameters and work to achieve individual goals
- groups usually operate by externally set procedures such as the traditional rules of order
- group members usually have separate roles and responsibilities and tend to work on their own
- individuals in groups operate at various levels of empowerment depending on their position in the organization
- little or no time is devoted to building relationships and issues of cohesion and trust are rarely systematically addressed
- groups rarely focus on feedback between members to improve group effectiveness
- leadership and decision-making power typically resides in the group chairperson

Since group members typically pursue their own individual goals, groups tend to exhibit "I"-centered behavior when debating. This generally makes a group more competitive and argumentative than a true team. When each person strives to get what's best for him- or herself, conflict tends to be handled in a more adversarial manner.

How Is a Team Different?

In contrast to a group, a team is a collection of people who come together to achieve a clear and compelling common goal that they have participated in defining. To the members of a true team, that goal is more important than their own individual pursuits. It's this factor that gives a team its cohesion.

A team also creates a set of norms or rules of conduct that define the team's culture. While a group may be run by a chairman, according to pre-published rules of order, a team runs itself by norms created by the members.

Team members also cooperate to plan and coordinate roles. Their work lives are linked together, and they depend on each other.

While all trout are fish, not all fish are trout! Likewise, all teams are groups, but not all groups are teams.

Teams have a common goal created by the members

It's important to know whether you're facilitating a team or a group.

When team members have differences of opinion, they tend to debate the ideas rather than argue points of view. They aren't out to gain personal victory, but to arrive at the best solution for the good of the whole.

While the members of a group generally have only the level of authority inherent in their position within the organization, teams seek and attain higher levels of empowerment. Drawing on each other to make better decisions, a team typically evolves toward greater autonomy in managing its work.

There is a definite sequence of stages a team goes through in order to reach high performance levels. A group does not tend to follow this pattern. One reason is that team membership is more permanent. While a group can operate with members coming and going, the members of a team need to be more consistent. In fact, if a member leaves a team, it may need to return briefly to the forming stage in order to integrate its new member.

Whether teams are created to stay together for just a few meetings or for years, they tend to develop more trust and openness than do most groups. Members have bought into the idea of working together and have made a commitment to common action. This helps create the comfort that many people need before they can freely express their ideas and concerns.

Group/Team Comparison Chart

A Group	A Team
Individual "I" focus	Collective "We" focus
Individual purpose	Common goal
Operates by external rules of order	Operates by own set of team norms
Operates alone	Has linked roles and responsibilities
Individuals have position authority	Seeks and gains empowerment
Meets irregularly	Meets regularly
Focuses on information sharing and coordinating	Focuses on problem solving and process improvement
Has a fixed chairperson	Shares leadership role
Fights to be right	Debates to make sound decisions
Is closed	Open and trusting
May like each other	Shares a strong bond

Do All Groups Need to Become Teams?

The simple answer is no. While teams have some distinct advantages over groups, not all groups should be developed into teams. A group should stay a group if:

- the members will only be together for a short time
- it's only supposed to do one simple task
- its purpose is solely to share information
- different members come to every meeting
- there's no regular or frequent pattern of meetings
- there's no real common goal or need for linked roles
- work is best planned and managed by isolated individuals
- there's no intent to empower
- there's no support for teamwork in the organization
- leadership styles are controlling and directive

Conversely, it's distinctly advantageous to do team building with any group if:

- there's a need to create a high level of cohesion and commitment to a common goal
- there's an ongoing task for the group to accomplish
- a consistent set of people will be working closely over an extended period
- members need to link and coordinate their roles closely
- higher empowerment levels will result in improved effectiveness and performance

As a facilitator, you should be aware that you'll probably work with more unstructured groups than real teams who have been through a team-building process. This is one of the factors that makes facilitation a challenge, since unschooled groups are likely to be unstructured, more argumentative and less skilled at effective interpersonal behaviors.

Getting a Group to Act Like a Team

Even when a group isn't destined to become a team, it's a good idea to take some tips from rudimentary team building and get members to at least act like a team while they're working together.

This can be achieved by incorporating the following key team building activities right into the agenda. These activities include:

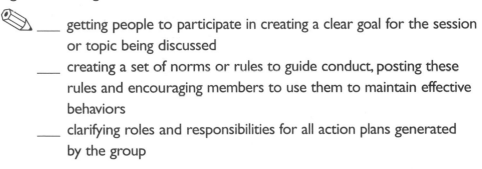 ___ getting people to participate in creating a clear goal for the session or topic being discussed

___ creating a set of norms or rules to guide conduct, posting these rules and encouraging members to use them to maintain effective behaviors

___ clarifying roles and responsibilities for all action plans generated by the group

Not all groups need to become teams, but . . .

. . . all groups can be encouraged to act like a team.

___ clarifying all accountabilities to insure that everyone is clear about expected results

___ training members in effective behaviors such as how to handle conflict and make decisions

___ conducting process checks, building in feedback loops and other evaluation mechanisms so that members can take responsibility for improving how the group functions

Understanding Team Stages

If you're working with a true team, you need to know that teams develop through four distinct stages. Each of these stages has unique characteristics and must be facilitated differently.

Forming

Forming is the first stage of team development. It starts when members are first brought together. In the forming stage, members tend to be optimistic and expectations are usually high. At the same time, there's also anxiety about fitting in and being able to achieve the task. Despite these early anxieties, forming is generally a "honeymoon" for most teams.

Members of forming teams are usually shy. They hold back until they know each other better. People are guarded with their comments. No one is sure exactly how he or she fits into the new team.

This stage is also characterized by an overdependence on the leader. Members want to be given a clear mandate, structure and parameters.

Forming can last anywhere from a few weeks to several months, depending on how often the team meets and how quickly the team completes the "team formation" agenda.

Facilitating the Formation of a Team

When facilitating a new team, you need to be optimistic and encouraging in order to ease anxieties. You also need to:

___ make sure there's clarity about the mandate and parameters for the new team

___ help the members collaborate to create a goal that achieves the stated mandate

___ break the ice with activities that create comfort and disclosure

___ help members develop norms or rules of conduct

___ identify tasks and specify roles and responsibilities

___ provide structure for all discussions

___ manage participation so that everyone has an equal say

___ provide training in decision making and effective behaviors

Forming teams requires context setting and relationship building.

Creating Team Norms

A major difference between groups and teams is that teams have clear norms or rules set by the team's members. These rules are used by the members to control their own and their peers' behaviors.

Developing norms is essential at the forming stage. Once they're in place, the norms are posted, referred to when behaviors become less than desirable and amended as the team matures.

Norms are always developed by team members. It only makes sense that bringing in norms from outside and asking the members to adhere to them will be largely ineffective. Members will be more likely to follow rules that they've created together.

Norms will vary somewhat with each team, but these are some of the most common:

- We will listen actively to all ideas
- Everyone's opinions count
- No interrupting while someone is talking
- Anyone can call "time out" if he or she feels the need for a break
- We will be open, yet honor privacy
- All team discussions will remain confidential
- We will respect differences
- We will be supportive rather than judgmental
- We will give helpful feedback directly and openly
- All team members will offer their ideas and resources
- Each member will take responsibility for the work of the team
- We will respect team meeting times by starting on time, returning from breaks promptly, avoiding unnecessary interruptions
- We will stay focused on our goals and avoid getting sidetracked
- When we have a difference of opinion, we'll debate the facts of the situation and not personalities
- We will all work to make sure there are no hidden agendas, and that all issues and concerns can be dealt with openly by all members

People are more likely to buy in to norms that they have created together.

Storming

Storming is a natural stage of team development and not necessarily a sign that you are an ineffective facilitator! In this stage, members experience a discrepancy between their initial hopes for the team and the realities of working together. Conflict arises and everyone knows that the honeymoon is over. Storming can take place for a variety of reasons, including:

Problems with the task: The task may be too difficult for members. Work loads may be unrealistic. Members may be resisting taking on more power and responsibility. The task itself may be unclear, or the members may not have bought into the task.

Storming is a natural stage.

Problems with the process: Lack of structure can cause any discussion to spin in circles.

Organizational barriers: Lots of storming is caused by inappropriate empowerment, lack of support and organizational barriers.

Lack of skills: If team members lack basic meeting and group effectiveness skills, they'll be unable to manage conflict or make difficult decisions. People may also lack skills in such things as problem solving, decision making or an important technical element of their job. Lack of skills is a major source of team storming.

Ineffective leadership: If a team leader is overly controlling while the members are trying to flex their muscles, members may challenge the leader in order to gain more power. Many traditional leaders are totally unfamiliar with team building and facilitation and hence unable to manage the stages of team growth.

Interpersonal conflict: People may discover that they like some members, but dislike others. Cliques can form. People may also clash over personal styles. Some people may not be pulling their weight. Others may talk too much or try to dominate. All of these interpersonal challenges contribute to team storming.

Beware of the Iceberg!

Many people mistakenly think that storming is essentially caused by interpersonal conflict. While conflict is a reliable sign of storming, think of it more as a symptom rather than the cause. In other words, be aware that people are often in conflict as a result of problems with the task, lack of process, skill gaps, ineffective leadership or organizational barriers.

Many factors contribute to storming.

Dysfunctional behavior is often a symptom of storming rather than its cause.

- Interpersonal conflict
- Problems with the task
- Lack of process/structure
- Lack of skills
- Ineffective leadership
- Organizational barriers

Reacting to Storming

During the storming phase it's common for members to feel dissatisfied with their dependence on someone else's authority, most often the team leader's. It's not unusual for members to challenge or even reject the leader at this stage. Power struggles can also take place among members who may be competing for authority.

Due to these various factors, the team may be distracted. As a result, productivity plummets. There's a feeling of ineffectiveness, and there may be meetings where little is achieved. Frustration increases. This is accompanied by a corresponding decline in morale. People start to wonder if the team is a good idea, since so much time seems to be wasted.

If you find yourself facilitating a team in storming, be careful not to take this personally. Check to see if this is what you're thinking:

> *"This is awful. Things are falling apart!"*
>
> *"They hate me! I hate them! I can't trust them!"*
>
> *"Who do they think they are? I'll fix them!"*

In order to survive storming, you need to believe:

> *"Storming is OK. It's a normal stage."*
>
> *"They don't hate me; they're just storming."*
>
> *"They don't hate each other; they're just storming."*
>
> *"This is energy I've got to channel into solutions."*
>
> *"We'll get through this together."*

Signs of Storming

Use the following checklist to raise your awareness of storming. It can help you determine whether the team you're working with is in this sensitive state:

- ___ the team isn't achieving its goals
- ___ people express frustration with blocks and barriers
- ___ people say the team makes them feel drained of energy
- ___ people no longer think the team is a good idea
- ___ there's no attention to process or how the team functions
- ___ there's a tendency toward arguing viewpoints instead of debating ideas
- ___ people don't listen actively or support each other's ideas
- ___ the team is divided into factions
- ___ members vie for power with and against each other
- ___ members demonstrate their lack of respect for the leader
- ___ meetings go in circles; little is achieved
- ___ there's a tendency to complain and second guess decisions
- ___ people are often late, absent or don't do their homework
- ___ no one wants to take responsibility; follow-through is poor
- ___ some people have withdrawn; they no longer participate
- ___ members go to each other after meetings to air their concerns

It's important not to take storming personally.

Facilitating a Team in Storming

Storming is the most difficult stage to facilitate because feelings are running high. Facilitators need to handle storming carefully in order to remain absolutely neutral and not take sides in any debates. Storming also demands a high degree of assertiveness on your part. Facilitators need to:

Storming is the hardest state to facilitate.

___ expect and accept tension as normal

___ stay totally neutral and calm

___ create an environment in which people can safely express feelings

___ honestly and openly admit that there's conflict

___ help members identify issues and solve them together

___ invite input and feedback

___ make interventions to correct dysfunctional behaviors

___ assertively referee heated discussions

___ train members in group skills

___ facilitate communication

When a Team Storms

There are two approaches for storming situations:

The outcome of storming depends on you!

BEST ACTIONS	WORST ACTIONS
↦ Surface all problems to get them on the table to be solved	↦ Ignore problems
↦ Create norms that make it safe to discuss problems. Encourage members to debate ideas in a non-personal way	↦ Avoid all arguments
↦ Offer clear options and encourage members to take control	↦ Take back control
↦ Help members identify strategies and action plans	↦ Tell people what to do
↦ Help members identify their problems and resolve them	↦ Take a punitive attitude

Norming

While norming is usually described as a team stage, it's actually a transitional step that moves a team from storming into performing. In norming, the team confronts its problems and resolves them. The resolutions that everyone agrees to become the new norms for the team.

During norming, members face their issues, accept feedback and act on it. This results in improvement in the team's performance.

There are four types of norming activities:

 ____ **Survey Feedback:** Create and circulate a survey that probes into the problems the group is experiencing. This could be a meeting effectiveness survey, a team effectiveness survey or a project progress survey. Return survey results to members for their analysis. Help members identify problems and implement remedial actions.

____ **Force-Field Analysis:** Facilitate a discussion in which members analyze what's working and what's not. Generate solutions for each item identified in the not-working category.

____ **Interpersonal Feedback:** Offer tools that allow members to give each other constructive feedback about what they're doing that's effective and what they could do better. This includes peer feedback and upward feedback to the leader.

____ **New Norm Development:** Help members review their existing norms and add any new norms that will help them be more effective. This can be done by turning the existing norms into a survey that lets members rate the extent to which each norm is being successfully applied.

The Facilitator's Role in Norming

If you're facilitating a group that's storming, you need to stop the team's work on the task and draw their attention to the process.

In norming it's essential that you stay totally neutral and offer the group tools with which they can solve their own problems. Key facilitator strategies include:

- offering feedback and inviting input
- encouraging problem identification and problem solving
- offering training and support to team members
- further sharing of power
- mediating in personality clashes
- coaching and counseling individuals
- encouraging others to take on leadership roles
- supporting members while they make improvements

Norming is a transitional activity more than a stage.

You exit storming and enter the norming phase when you stop members and ask them to assess how they're doing with the aim of improving the team's effectiveness.

Performing—The Final Team Growth Stage

If norming is managed successfully, team members will create new norms and action steps that help them perform more effectively. Once the main blocks and barriers have been removed, members will be ready to focus on their work without distraction. Everyone wins here. Productivity goes up. So does morale. Once the a team reaches the performing stage, you will notice that:

- time and resources are used efficiently; more work gets done
- everyone behaves in a supportive way
- everyone shares power by rotating leadership roles
- members take turns facilitating
- members feel committed and bonded
- the official leader is treated as a valued member
- the team evaluates and corrects continuously
- decisions made are typically high-quality
- conflicts are seen as constructive debates, rarely getting heated or emotional

All performing teams have:

1. A clear team goal that has been created by the team and that dovetails with organizational targets
2. Established ground rules or norms that are adjusted regularly and used to monitor and improve the team
3. Detailed work plans that define tasks, clarify roles and responsibilities, lay out a schedule of events and specify the performance expectations of the team
4. Clearly defined empowerment so that members know which decisions they can make
5. Clear and open communication between members and with those outside the team
6. Well-defined decision-making procedures that help the team know which decision-making approach to use
7. Beneficial team behaviors that reflect good interpersonal skills and positive intent to make the team successful
8. Balanced participation so that everyone is heard and the team's decision making isn't dominated by one or two strong personalities
9. Awareness of group process along with regular initiatives to improve how the team functions
10. Well-planned and executed meetings with detailed agendas

Facilitating a Performing Team

You'll find that the easiest group to facilitate is a high-performance team whose members have learned to manage their own conflict and who have highly developed interpersonal skills. But that doesn't mean your job's over yet. In these situations you need to:

___ collaborate with members more to get their input

___ share facilitation duties

___ offer expertise to the team

___ help the team reward and celebrate success

___ offer to observe and give feedback to further improve the team

Facilitation Strategies Chart

Use the following quick reference to match appropriate facilitator approaches with the team-development stage being experienced by the group or team.

Stage	Key Elements	Facilitator Strategies
Group	May be strangers "I"- focused individuals Lack of compelling goal No norms Roles loosely linked Individual accountabilities	Warm-up exercises Build buy-in Create a common goal Create and use norms Clarify and link roles Define accountabilities Teach interpersonal skills Provide clear process Encourage participation Evaluate meeting effectiveness

Main Strategy—To provide structure and support

Stage	Key Elements	Facilitator Strategies
Forming	Members unsure Uncertainty Low trust Need direction Commitment low Group skills unrefined Overdependence on leader	Warm-up exercises Disclosure exercises Build buy-in Create a common goal Create and use norms Define accountabilities Clarify roles and responsibilities Provide clear process Encourage participation Evaluate team effectiveness

*Main Strategy—Build team spirit and comfort while
providing lots of structure for activities*

High-performing teams are the easiest to facilitate.

Groups tend to lack cohesion and are prone to "I-centered" behavior.

New teams need clear parameters and relationship building activities.

Storming is the "make it or break it" stage.

Stage	Key Elements	Facilitator Strategies
Storming	Problems with the task	Expect and accept tension
	Lack of process	Stay neutral and calm
	Lack of skills	Create safety for expressing
	Ineffective leadership	feelings
	Blocks and barriers	Honestly admit there's conflict
	Cliques form	Help members identify and
	Conflict emerges	solve issues
	Frustration sets in	Invite input and feedback
	Animosities develop	Make interventions
	Leader is rejected	Assertively referee conflict
	Power struggles	Teach interpersonal and
	Emotional arguing	conflict management skills
		Encourage communication

*Main Strategy—To listen, address conflict,
referee assertively and resolve issues collaboratively*

Norming requires honesty and disclosure.

Stage	Key Elements	Facilitator Strategies
Norming	Members "own" problems	Offer methods for feedback
	Conflicts are resolved	Help solve problems
	Power issues are resolved	Invite personal feedback
	Team redefines its norms	Offer further training
	Performance problems	Support members while they
	corrected	make improvements
	Create empowerment plans	Share power
		Mediate personality clashes
		Coach and counsel individuals
		Share the leadership role

*Main Strategy—To help the group refocus and
support team improvement efforts*

Performing teams can manage their own process.

Stage	Key Elements	Facilitator Strategies
Performing	High productivity	Collaborate with members
	Conflicts managed by	on process
	members	Rotate facilitation duties
	High commitment to goal	Offer your expertise
	Roles and responsibilities	Help the team recognize and
	clear	celebrate success
	Members behave in a	
	facilitative manner	
	Team continuously	
	improves itself	
	Members feel committed	
	and bonded	

*Main Strategy—To build agendas together, share facilitation
responsibilities, collaborate, act as a resource*

Team Effectiveness Survey

Provide your candid opinion of your immediate work team by rating its key characteristics on the five-point scale shown below. Circle the appropriate number on each scale to represent your evaluation. Do not put your name on this. Return the survey in the envelope provided.

Administer a team survey periodically, then use the steps of the survey-feedback process to identify improvement strategies.

1. Goal Clarity
Are goals and objectives clearly understood and accepted by all members?

1	2	3	4	5

Goals and objectives aren't known, understood or accepted   Goals and objectives are clear and accepted

2. Participation
Is everyone involved and heard during group discussions or is there a "tyranny of a minority"?

1	2	3	4	5

A few people tend to dominate   Everyone is active and has a say

3. Consultation
Are team members consulted on matters concerning them?

1	2	3	4	5

We are seldom consulted   Team members are always consulted

4. Decision Making
Is the group both objective and effective at making decisions?

1	2	3	4	5

The team is ineffective at at reaching decisions   The team is very effective reaching decisions

5. Roles and Responsibilities
When action is planned, are clear assignments made and accepted?

1	2	3	4	5

Roles are poorly defined   Roles are clearly defined

6. Procedures
Does the team have clear rules, methods and procedures to guide it? Are there agreed-upon methods for problem solving?

1	2	3	4	5

There is little structure and we lack procedures   The team has clear rules and procedures

Team Effectiveness Survey, cont'd

7. Communications

Are communications between members open and honest? Do members listen actively?

1	2	3	4	5

Communications are not open
Not enough listening

Communications are open
People listen

8. Confronting Difficulties

Are difficult or uncomfortable issues openly worked through or are conflicts avoided? Are conflicts worked through?

1	2	3	4	5

Difficulties are avoided
Little direct conflict management

Problems are attacked
openly and directly

9. Openness & Trust

Are team members open in their transactions? Are there hidden agendas? Do members feel free to be candid?

1	2	3	4	5

Individuals are guarded
and hide motives

Everyone is open and
speaks freely

10. Commitment

How committed are team members to deadlines, meetings and other team activities?

1	2	3	4	5

Deadlines and commitments
often missed

Total commitment

11. Support

Do members pull for each other? What happens when one person makes a mistake? Do members help each other?

1	2	3	4	5

Little evidence of support

Lots of support

12. Risk Taking

Do individuals feel that they can try new things, risk failure? Does the team encourage risk?

1	2	3	4	5

Little support for risk

Lots of support for risk

13. Atmosphere

Is the team atmosphere informal, comfortable and relaxed?

1	2	3	4	5

The team spirit is tense   The team is
                                                     comfortable and relaxed

14. Leadership

Are leadership roles shared, or do the same people dominate and control?

1	2	3	4	5

A few people dominate   Leadership is evenly shared

15. Evaluation

Does the team routinely stop and evaluate how it's doing in order to improve?

1	2	3	4	5

We never evaluate   We routinely evaluate

16. Meetings

Are meetings orderly, well planned and productive?

1	2	3	4	5

Waste of time   Couldn't be better

17. Fun

Is there an "esprit de corps," or sense of fun, on this team?

1	2	3	4	5

Humbug!   We have fun!

Notes

Chapter 4
Creating Participation

*I*magine yourself at the start of a day-long session with a group of people you barely know and nothing is working. No one is answering questions. Some people look bored. Others seem openly uncomfortable. Everyone looks nervously at the leader whenever you ask a serious question. You start to wonder how you're going to get through the rest of the session!

Given the pressures of today's workplace, it would be naive to go into most meetings assuming that people will automatically be enthusiastic and engaged.

The first step in getting people to participate actively is to understand why they may be holding back. Consider these barriers to participation:

_____ people may be tired from attending too many meetings

_____ some participants may be exhausted from overwork

_____ some members may be confused about the topic being discussed

_____ there may be a lack of commitment to the topic of the meeting

_____ some people may be insecure about speaking in front of others

_____ talkative members may "shut down" quieter people

_____ junior staff may be reluctant to speak up in front of those they consider to be their "superiors"

_____ there may be a low level of trust and openness in the group

_____ some traumatic event may have occurred recently that has left people feeling stressed or withdrawn

_____ the organization may have a history of not listening to or supporting employee suggestions

When planning any session, it's important to assess how participative the members are likely to be. Before the workshop, find out:

_____ whether or not the participants are used to group discussion

_____ how committed people are to the topic

_____ how the members feel about speaking in front of their leader and each other

_____ whether relations between participants are healthy or strained

_____ if there has been a recent layoff, personal tragedy or other event that might distract participants

_____ if members have well-developed group skills such as listening, debating, decision making, etc.

_____ whether the organization is likely to support the ideas of the group

Anticipate the potential blocks to active participation and come armed with strategies to overcome them.

Creating the Conditions for Full Participation

Understand what it takes for people to open up.

As a facilitator you need to understand the basic prerequisites for full participation. In general, people will participate fully if they:

- ____ feel relaxed with the other participants
- ____ understand the topic under discussion
- ____ have had some say in the planning process
- ____ feel committed to the topic
- ____ have the information and knowledge needed for fruitful discussion
- ____ feel safe in expressing their opinions
- ____ aren't interfered with or otherwise unduly influenced
- ____ trust and have confidence in the facilitator
- ____ are comfortable and at ease in the meeting room
- ____ feel that the organization will support their ideas

A good rule is that the more resistant a group is likely to be, the more necessary it is to hold interviews or focus groups with members beforehand to let them voice their concerns and become aware of their blocks.

Removing the Blocks to Participation

Ensuring that people participate actively is one of your primary responsibilities. There's no excuse for running a meeting that a few people dominate or in which half the group sits in silent withdrawal. Here are some strategies to encourage involvement.

Break the Ice

Always have a few ice-breakers in mind.

Even in a group in which members know one another, they need to engage in ice breakers to set a warm and supportive tone. With groups of strangers, ice breakers are even more important. They help people get to know each other and help to remove barriers to speaking in front of strangers.

Books on ice breakers abound. Do your homework so that you have at least four to six simple warm-up exercises handy at all times.

Clarify the Topic

Clarify the purpose and outcome of each discussion.

At the start of each discussion, take pains to insure that each topic is clearly defined. For example, if the meeting is being called to solve a problem, insure that there's a clear problem statement. Regardless of the type of session, a clear statement that describes the purpose of the meeting is a must.

You add to topic clarity by having a well-defined outcome statement for each discussion. This means helping the group to agree on what they hope to achieve. This aligns the participants.

At the start of any session, make sure everyone is clear about the purpose of the meeting by:

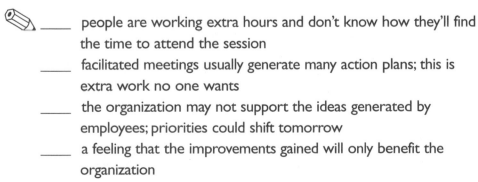

_____ reviewing what created the need for the meeting so that everyone understands its history

_____ sharing the input members gave during surveys, focus groups or interviews to demonstrate member participation in creating the agenda

_____ engaging participants in ratifying a purpose statement to insure understanding and commitment

_____ stating the goal of the facilitation so everyone is clear about the desired outcome

Always be alert to the fact that even a crystal clear purpose can quickly become cloudy. Members can get sidetracked or suddenly decide there's a more important issue to be discussed. Performing effectively in your role means checking often to make sure that members remain clear about the goal and haven't become confused. This may lead to the realization that the group has indeed been marching down the wrong road and now needs to redefine the goal and potentially start over in a new direction.

It's quite common for facilitators to have to redesign a session in midstream. That's what makes facilitating such a challenge! The wise facilitator is always open to making changes. Forcing a group to continue a discussion that no longer makes sense, just because it's on the agenda, is a sure formula for disaster.

Even a clear purpose can become obscure.

Create Buy-In

In many organizations speculation about layoffs is rampant. People may also be weary after wave upon wave of new initiatives. These and other forms of turbulence have left people cynical. They feel vulnerable and abused. They work longer hours for less pay. In many organizations, employee morale is at an all-time low, while distrust of management is high.

Facilitators who naively think that people are automatically going to be keen and enthusiastic about coming to their session are in for a shock. These days it's especially important to check with your group to determine how many of the following harsh realities are going to be a factor:

Never assume that people are automatically bought in!

_____ people are working extra hours and don't know how they'll find the time to attend the session

_____ facilitated meetings usually generate many action plans; this is extra work no one wants

_____ the organization may not support the ideas generated by employees; priorities could shift tomorrow

_____ a feeling that the improvements gained will only benefit the organization

In today's work environment, you'd be foolish to attempt to run any meeting without gaining commitment and buy-in from the participants.

Getting people to commit is achieved by asking them to answer the universal buy-in question: *"What's in it for me?"*

An effective buy-in activity is to pair up participants at the start of any session and ask them to spend several minutes discussing two questions:

> *"What's the gain for the organization?"*
> *"How will you personally benefit?"*

Incorporate the buy-in process at the start of major meetings.

After the partner discussion, participants can recount their own or their partner's responses. Record all comments on a flip chart. The responses to the second question amount to the participant's psychological buy-in to the session. This seems deceptively simple, but is actually a powerful conversation.

If participants say there are few benefits but lots of reasons for them not to participate, you'll need to spend more time on the buy-in activity.

In these cases of heightened levels of resistance, add two additional questions to the partner buy-in exercise:

> *"What's blocking me personally from participating? Why might I be reluctant?"*

> *"What will it take to overcome these blocks? Under what conditions, and with what support, will I consider giving this my total commitment?"*

When you record member responses to these two additional questions, you're actually negotiating their participation. People may say they'll participate if there are assurances that senior management will support their ideas or that they'll receive training or other needed assistance. Having their conditions on the table lets you assess the extent to which participants are feeling blocked.

The problem with identifying the blocks is, of course, that you may not be in a position to negotiate some of these items. If you anticipate strong resistance, it's best to surface the blocks in the planning phase. This allows you time to negotiate support issues before the session. The results of these negotiations can then be presented at the beginning of the session to help relieve concerns and help people move forward with commitment. In high-resistance situations, managers and even senior managers may have to be present at the start of a meeting to respond to the needs described by the members.

Vary the buy-in question for different situations. To create "buy-in" for a process-improvement exercise, ask members:

> *"How will my work life be made easier if we manage to simplify this process?"*

To create "buy-in" for joining a team, ask group members:

> *"What are the benefits for me personally, if I become a member of this team?"*

To create "buy-in" for learning a new skill, ask group members:
> *"How is learning to operate the new software going to benefit me?"*

Make Eye Contact

This is a simple but a very important technique to improve participation. Facilitators need to make eye contact with *everyone*, not just the active participants. By looking directly at quiet people, you're telling them that they haven't been forgotten. Sometimes your glance will prompt them to speak up. The eye contact must, of course, be friendly and encouraging, not piercing and intimidating.

Use eye contact to include quiet people.

Use Humor

Everybody enjoys a good laugh, especially these days. Humor is a great way to create an open atmosphere. How to introduce humor into your session? Have people reveal an amusing anecdote about themselves, show cartoons or stop periodically for a team game. Running jokes and amusing comments are all useful as long as they're in proper proportion and don't detract from the focus of the session.

Humor needs to be in proper proportion.

Manage the Participation of Leaders

If you're acting as an external facilitator, you'll often be asked to plan and manage meetings in which the group's leader is present. This leader may be the person who contacted you and who considers him- or herself to be your client.

Leaders are often used to chairing meetings and influencing their outcome. It isn't unheard of for a leader to ask a facilitator to lead a discussion in the direction of a predetermined outcome he or she favors. The harsh reality is that some people see facilitation as a sophisticated tool for manipulating others.

To avoid misunderstandings, the facilitator and leader need to meet ahead of time to discuss a number of key points. The leader needs to be tactfully told that:

Some leaders need to be coached ahead of time not to dominate.

- the leader isn't the client; a facilitator's client is always the whole group, including the leader
- facilitation is a democratic undertaking in which the leader accepts decisions made by the whole group
- the facilitator needs to be able to contact participants before the session, via interviews or surveys to gain their input

If the pre-session interviews with staff reveal that the leader is domineering or that staff are reluctant to speak in the leader's presence, it's a wise strategy to speak with the leader before the session and ask him or her to hold back. Every experienced facilitator can recount stories of situations in which he or she had to take the group leader aside at a break and ask him or her to temper their participation.

It may be a strategy to have the leader attend a kick-off session, pledge support and then leave while the staff work. At the end of the session, the leader returns to hear final recommendations, give any needed approvals and offer to act as an ongoing sponsor of member activities.

If you're lucky enough to have a group whose leader is open and regarded as a valuable colleague by team members, encourage him or her to play an active role in the entire discussion. After all, one of the reasons leaders bring in facilitators is so they can participate and offer their expertise to the group.

People won't participate if they haven't done their homework.

Some discussions require special norms

Help Participants Prepare

People often hold back at meetings because they aren't prepared. To prevent this from happening in your sessions, make sure that the purpose of the meeting is clearly communicated so that people have time to prepare. If the meeting is expected to be complex, identify who needs to do which portion of the homework. When people do adequate pre-work, they gain confidence and participate more actively.

Create Targeted Norms

All groups need guidelines to insure a cooperative and supportive climate. As mentioned on page 57 of this book, norms should be written by the participants themselves. Having a basic set of norms may not, however, be sufficient to handle the task of getting through a sensitive conversation.

If the conversation the group is about to have is sensitive in nature, the group will need to create specific, targeted norms to insure that members feel safe enough to participate. Safety norms are an example of targeted norms. In this case, norms are created for the comfort of participants who may feel that they're operating in a particularly sensitive environment.

Help members create safety norms by asking these questions:
"What rules should we establish today that will insure everyone feels he or she can speak up with confidence? Under what conditions are you going to be able to say what's on your mind?"

Some sample safety norms are:

- all ideas will be listened to carefully
- all discussions will be held strictly confidential: "what's said here, stays here"
- both people and issues will be handled with respect and sincerity
- there will be no retaliation on the basis of anything that is said in this meeting
- no one will personally attack another person
- all feedback must be phrased in a constructive manner and be aimed at helping the other person
- if anyone feels emotionally stressed they can call time out or request a change in how a topic is being handled
- everyone will use neutral body language and avoid things like finger-pointing, eye rolling or sighing
- instead of arguing personal points, we will listen to and acknowledge each other's ideas first
- anyone can call a time out if he or she is confused about the topic or feels that the discussion is going off track

Targeted norms may also be necessary in a variety of other situations.

- If **conflict** is anticipated, ask a norming question such as:
  "What rules do we need to set today to insure we effectively manage differences of opinion at this meeting?"

- If any members of the group are **reluctant to participate**, ask:
  "What guidelines should we establish that will encourage participation and help all members feel their ideas are important?"

- If the group has trouble **staying on track**, ask:
  "What rules will help insure that we stay on track and on time today?"

As with regular norms, targeted norms need to be developed by the participants, in response to specific situations. If there's no response when you ask the norming question, divide members into pairs or subgroups to answer the norming question. Then, gather up their ideas.

Set Up the Room to Encourage Participation

It's a factor that may not seem major at first, but how you arrange a room will greatly affect how group members interact. Theater-style seating is the worst possible arrangement for facilitating an active discussion. People automatically assume that they'll be spoken at. It also discourages people from looking at each other.

Large boardroom tables have an especially stifling effect on people. This is very unfortunate, as many large companies have huge boardroom tables stuck squarely in the middle of their best meeting room. If this room is your only option, break people into pairs, trios and foursomes as often as possible to keep everyone talking.

If you have any choice in the matter of seating, select a large room and try to get small, modular tables. Small rectangles arranged in a large horseshoe for whole group sessions or smaller squares for small group discussions are the best.

If the group has more than ten people, break it into small groups of not more than eight people per group. People can sit in their small groups, even when the whole group is in session. Small groups always help break the ice and create a more private forum for discussions.

Clarify Your Role

People sometimes hold back if they're confused about your role. Near the beginning of any facilitation, tell participants why you're there and what you'll be doing. Be clear that you'll make sure everyone is heard, that you'll work hard to keep discussions on track and that you'll be remaining neutral on all topics.

Share your hopes for a successful meeting, so people know you intend to help make it a productive session. Don't be afraid to brag about yourself a bit. Some participants will be more likely to speak up if they have confidence in your skills.

Creating the right norms will encourage people to participate.

Seat people to encourage conversation.

Be clear about your process role.

Identify the Organizational Supports

If the pre-workshop interviews reveal that people are worried that the session might be an exercise in futility, be sure to express these concerns to the appropriate manager. There is nothing worse than having members balk at the start of a workshop because they're worried that their ideas won't be supported. If organizational barriers can be dealt with before the session, that will help create a much more positive environment.

Another common strategy is to have a senior manager attend the kick-off portion of the meeting to offer his or her personal assurance of support for the group's efforts. If this isn't possible, a memo or letter from the senior manager expressing strong support is a help.

If there's no senior management support and barriers are a major concern, it's important to surface these issues and discuss them, rather than pretend they don't exist. Set aside time at the end of the workshop to identify the barriers, analyze them and generate solutions for getting around them. This way members will feel that the discussions have been honest and that they have strategies for dealing with the realities they face.

Recognize past frustrations that members have had with organizational blocks.

High-Participation Techniques

There are many excellent techniques available to get even the most reluctant and shy participant to play an active part. These techniques offer anonymity to members and generate lots of energy.

Discussion Partners

This simple technique can be used as a way of starting any discussion. After posing a question to a large group, ask everyone to find a partner to discuss the question for a few minutes. Have people report on what they talked about. You can use this with threesomes as well.

Use diads to get people talking.

Tossed Salad

Place an empty cardboard box or an inexpensive plastic salad bowl on the table. Give out small slips of paper and ask people to write down one good idea per slip. Have them toss the slips into the bowl. When people have finished writing, have someone "toss the salad." Pass around the bowl so that each person can take out as many slips as they tossed in. Go around the table and have people share ideas before discussing and refining the most promising ideas as a group.

Allow for anonymity.

Issues and Answers

When faced with a long list of issues to tackle, rather than attempting to problem solve all of them as a whole group, which may take too long, post the problems around the room. Put only one issue on each sheet of flip chart paper.

Ask all members to go to one of the issue sheets and discuss that problem with whomever else was drawn to that sheet. Make sure people are distributed evenly, with at least three people per issue. You can use chairs, but this works best as a stand-up activity.

Allow up to five minutes for the subgroups to analyze the situation. Have them make notes on the top half of the flip chart sheet. Ring a bell and ask everyone to move to another flip chart sheet. When they get there, ask them to read the analysis made by the first group and to add any additional ideas. This round is often shorter than five minutes. Keep people circulating until everyone has added to all of the sheets.

Once the analysis round is complete, ask everyone to return to the original issue he or she started with. Ask them to generate and record solutions to their respective issue on the bottom half of the sheet. Once again circulate people until everyone has added ideas on all of the sheets.

To end the process have everyone walk by each sheet, read all of the solutions and check off the one to three ideas they think are best.

When everyone has returned to their seats, review the top rated ideas and then ask small groups to take responsibility for creating action plans.

Talk Circuit

This technique works best in a large crowd because it creates a strong buzz and lets people get to know each other. Start by posing a question to the group and then allow quiet time for each person to write his or her own response.

Ask everyone to sit "knee to knee" with a partner and share their ideas. Have one person speak while the other acts as facilitator. After two to three minutes ring a bell and have partners reverse their roles. After two or three more minutes stop the discussions.

Ask everyone to find a new partner and repeat the process, but in slightly less time. Stop the action and then have everyone repeat the process with a third partner.

In the final round allow only one minute per person. When the partner discussions are over, share the ideas as a whole group and record them on flip charts.

Pass the Envelope

Give each person an envelope filled with blank slips of paper. Pose a question or challenge to the group, and then have everyone write down as many ideas as they can within the given time frame and put the slips into the envelope. Tell people to pass the envelopes, either to the next person or in all directions, and when the passing stops, read the contents. Pair off participants and have them discuss the ideas in their envelope. What ideas did they receive? What are the positives and negatives of each idea? What other ideas should they add? Combine pairs to form groups of four and ask them to further refine the content of their four envelopes into practical action plans. Hold a plenary to collect ideas.

Use the walls!

Partner people with those they know the least.

Use anonymous brainstorming.

Group Participation Survey

Please review the following statements and rate how your group currently manages the participation of members. Be totally honest. Remember that this survey is anonymous. The results will be tabulated and fed back to the group for their assessment.

1. People feel free to express any idea regardless of who is present

1	2	3	4	5
totally disagree	disagree somewhat	not sure	agree somewhat	totally agree

2. Everyone feels totally relaxed

1	2	3	4	5
totally disagree	disagree somewhat	not sure	agree somewhat	totally agree

3. Everyone is clear about the purpose

1	2	3	4	5
totally disagree	disagree somewhat	not sure	agree somewhat	totally agree

4. Everyone has done their homework and is prepared

1	2	3	4	5
totally disagree	disagree somewhat	not sure	agree somewhat	totally agree

5. Members listen to and respect each other's views

1	2	3	4	5
totally disagree	disagree somewhat	not sure	agree somewhat	totally agree

6. Members appreciate each other's different strengths. Everyone is valued for his or her specific skills

1	2	3	4	5
totally disagree	disagree somewhat	not sure	agree somewhat	totally agree

7. Members recognize and accept individual differences

1	2	3	4	5
totally disagree	disagree somewhat	not sure	agree somewhat	totally agree

8. The organization fully supports the work of the group

1	2	3	4	5
totally disagree	disagree somewhat	not sure	agree somewhat	totally agree

Encouraging Effective Meeting Behaviors

Sometimes you'll find yourself working with groups whose members behave as though they were being paid bonuses for rudeness. People interrupt. Members run in and out. People dismiss ideas before they've really tried to understand them, and so on.

Producing outcomes is a battle in these situations. Sometimes the wisest thing to do is stop the proceedings and raise member awareness about effective meeting behaviors.

This mini-training session is simple, quick and surprisingly effective. It consists of the following steps:

1. Introduce the idea that certain behaviors are less effective than others. Hand out the sheets on the next two pages, which describe effective and ineffective meeting behaviors. Review each behavior. Answer any questions.

2. Ask all members to act as observers for the rest of the meeting. Give each person an observation sheet and ask them to make note of all occurrences of the listed behaviors. This means keeping track of both the names of people and the specific thing done or said.

3. At the end of the session, set aside some time to share observations.
   "Were there more effective or ineffective behaviors displayed?"
   "Which ineffective behaviors were in evidence?"

4. At the end of this discussion, help group members to write new norms by asking:
   "What new rules should be added to the existing norms to overcome these behaviors?"

Never continue facilitating a session in which people behave dysfunctionally!

Group Behaviors Handout

Behaviors That Help Effectiveness:

Behavior	Description
Listens Actively	looks at the person who is speaking, nods, asks probing questions and acknowledges what is said by paraphrasing point(s) made
Supports	encourages others to develop ideas and make suggestions; gives them recognition for their ideas
Probes	goes beyond the surface comments by questioning teammates to uncover hidden information
Clarifies	asks members for more information about what they mean; clears up confusion
Offers Ideas	shares suggestions, ideas, solutions and proposals
Includes Others	asks quiet members for their opinions, making sure no one is left out
Summarizes	pulls together ideas from a number of people; determines where the group is and what has been covered
Harmonizes	reconciles opposing points of view; links together similar ideas; points out where ideas are the same
Manages Conflict	listens to the views of others; clarifies issues and key points made by opponents; seeks solutions

Behaviors That Hinder Effectiveness

Behavior	Description
"Yeah But's"	discredits the ideas of others
Blocks	insists on getting one's way; doesn't compromise; stands in the way of the team's progress
Grandstands	draws attention to one's personal skills; boasts
Goes Off Topic	directs the conversation off onto other topics
Dominates	tries to "run" the group through dictating, bullying
Withdraws	doesn't participate or offer help or support to others
Devil's Advocate	takes pride in being contrary
Criticizes	makes negative comments about people or their ideas
Personal Slurs	hurls insults at other people

Observing Group Behaviors in Action

EFFECTIVE	INEFFECTIVE
Actively listens	*Yeah but's*
Supports	*Blocks*
Probes	*Grandstands*
Clarifies	*Goes off topic*
Offers ideas	*Dominates*
Includes others	*Withdraws*
Summarizes	*Devil's advocate*
Harmonizes	*Criticizes*
Manages conflict	*Personal slurs*

Peer Review

There are times when group members need to receive feedback from each other. This may be necessary when they're experiencing conflict or when individuals are letting down the team.

The peer feedback format consists of two areas of focus, both of which have a positive intent. The first lets people praise each other. The second offers supportive advice to help the other person improve. These areas are:

1. *"What you do that's really effective. Keep on doing it!"*

2. *"What you could do that would make you even more effective."*

Here's how everyone can participate in this powerful feedback exercise:

Step 1: Each member writes his or her name at the top of a blank Peer Review Format worksheet on the next page and then passes it to the right.

Step 2: Each member answers both questions about the person whose name is at the top of each sheet.

Step 3: Sheets are passed around the table until everyone has written comments about each member.

Step 4: Each person eventually gets back the sheet with his or her own name on it, completely filled out with comments from all of the other members.

Step 5: The process can stop here, with each person keeping his or her own feedback, or you can ask people to:
- pass the completed sheets around again, and have people read aloud the positive comments they wrote about the other person. This is called a "strength bombardment."
- Have members choose partners to discuss what they learned from their feedback and create action plans for personal change. End with members sharing their action steps with the group.

This form of peer review is non-threatening, because no one receives negative comments, as both feedback questions are positive and forward-looking.

This exercise is extremely effective because the coaching advice is coming from peers. It subtly reminds members of the importance of meeting each other's needs and expectations. If tensions develop between people, this feedback method allows them to safely request what they need from each other. Since peer feedback often resolves interpersonal conflicts before they flare up, it's a good activity to do periodically as a preventative measure.

Harness the power of peer feedback to manage member behaviors.

Peer Review Worksheet

Name: _____ Date: _____

What you do that's really effective. Keep on doing it!

What you could do that would make you even more effective.

✎ Notes

Chapter 5
Effective Decision Making

Helping groups make high quality decisions is one of the most important functions of a facilitator. It's also one of the most difficult! There are a number of things that make decision making such a challenge:

- people may be trying to make a decision without having done their homework or being in possession of all of the important facts
- the key stakeholders or decision-makers may not be present
- individuals in the group may have a solution or position in mind that they spend their time advocating without being open to further input
- a few people may dominate while others hold their ideas back
- there may be real confusion about the purpose of the decision-making conversation or whether the group is empowered to decide the issue under discussion
- there may be no process in place to give the conversation structure, so the group engages in unstructured thrashing that's more emotional and subjective than it is factual and objective
- frustration may cause group members to give up their quest for a solution and resort to voting or simply moving on to the next topic without closure

To insure that you're always facilitating high quality decision processes, become aware of the traits of effective decision making:

- everyone is clear about the purpose of the decision-making conversation
- the group knows the extent of its power to make the decision in question
- the right people are there
- people have done their homework and possess the relevant data
- there's a clear structure for making the decision: people understand the approach to be taken and are willing to follow it
- there's an objective and open atmosphere in which ideas are exchanged and considered
- everyone at the meeting is viewed as important and no one person or sub-group dominates
- if the decision process becomes deadlocked, group members stop and examine why they're stuck and seek ways of ending the impasse
- the discussion ends with a real sense of closure and clear next steps

Helping groups make high-quality decisions is the most important function of a facilitator.

Know the Four Types of Conversations

The first step in being able to support effective decision making is awareness that conversations fall into one of the following categories:

Information sharing—this involves things like giving update reports, reviewing items from previous meetings or making lists for later ranking. Note that brainstorming falls into this category and is not a decision-making discussion. Information sharing discussions are chaired, rather than facilitated and result in little collaboration amongst participants.

Groups tend to share information. Teams do more of the other three things.

Planning—this involves participants in such activities as visioning and creating goal statements, describing objectives and expected results, assessing needs, identifying priorities and creating detailed action steps. Budget planning and program planning discussions fall into this category. Managed change initiatives are also planning activities. Lots of decisions get made during planning conversations, thus they require structure and active facilitation to insure input from members.

Problem solving—encompasses activities that engage participants in identifying and resolving issues together. The core activities involve gathering data, identifying problems, analyzing the current situation, using criteria to sort potential solutions and planning for action. Customer service initiatives and process improvement projects fall into this category. Since it results in actions that create change, problem solving also needs to be carefully structured and systematically facilitated.

Relationship building—this includes activities that help people get to know each other and build cohesion. This inculdes activities such as ice breakers, norm development sessions and conflict mediations. Structured team building sessions are an example of relationship building discussions. Important agreements are made during relationship building discussions, so they also need to be carefully structured and assertively facilitated.

Always identify if the purpose of a discussion is to make decisions or simply to share information.

At the start of each conversation, facilitators need to determine which of the four discussions is taking place and whether or not the group is making decisions:

If it's information sharing, list making or brainstorming:	If it's planning, problem solving or relationship building:
– no decisions will be made	– decisions will be made
– facilitation isn't critical	– a clear process is needed
– synergy isn't important	– facilitation is important
– closure is not needed	– people need to build on each other's thoughts
– next steps optional	– closure and clear next steps are needed

The Four Levels of Empowerment

Once you're clear about the type of discussion to be held, clarify the level of empowerment at which a decision is being made and communicate that information to members at the start of any decision-making discussion.

Nothing causes greater confusion and distrust than a lack of clarity about empowerment levels. It's very common for groups to assume that they have final say in making a decision, while management is merely asking for their opinion as input to a decision that managers will be making later.

When empowerment is unclear, people jump to conclusions and make assumptions. The most common mistaken assumption is that empowerment always means total control. Fortunately, empowerment doesn't have to be a confusing concept when you use the following four-level empowerment model.

It's essential to clarify empowerment levels.

The Empowerment Continuum

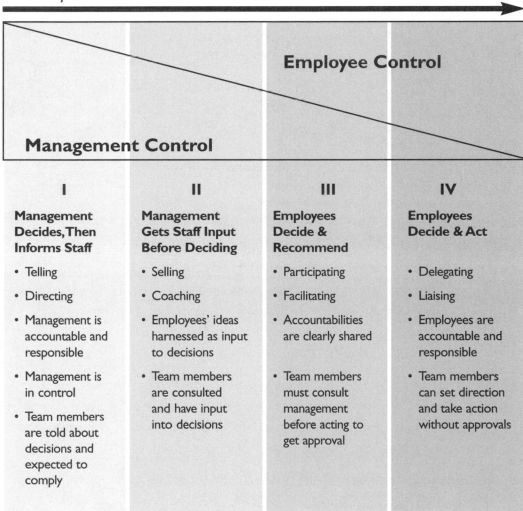

Share the empowerment chart with participants.

I	II	III	IV
Management Decides, Then Informs Staff	**Management Gets Staff Input Before Deciding**	**Employees Decide & Recommend**	**Employees Decide & Act**
• Telling	• Selling	• Participating	• Delegating
• Directing	• Coaching	• Facilitating	• Liaising
• Management is accountable and responsible	• Employees' ideas harnessed as input to decisions	• Accountabilities are clearly shared	• Employees are accountable and responsible
• Management is in control	• Team members are consulted and have input into decisions	• Team members must consult management before acting to get approval	• Team members can set direction and take action without approvals
• Team members are told about decisions and expected to comply			

Clarifying the Four Empowerment Levels

Level I—this refers to any decision made by management without input from employees. Employees are informed of the decision and expected to comply

Level II—this is a decision made by management after seeking input from employees. Employees are consulted but have no actual say in the final outcome and are expected to comply. An employee focus group is an example of a level II decision-making process

Level III—in this category of decision, employees discuss and recommend a course of action, but are unable to act without gaining final approval. Problem-solving workshops are often set up as level III activities

Level IV—in this level of decision, the group has been given full authority to make a decision and implement action plans without having to seek further approvals.

It's the role of the facilitator to help group members determine the extent of their empowerment in each decision-making activity by asking:

- *"Are you being told the decision, or is it going to be made elsewhere?" (Level I)*
- *"Are you being asked for your opinion?" (Level II)*
- *"Are you making recommendations that require further approval before acting?" (Level III)*
- *"Are you fully able to go ahead and implement whatever decision is made by the group?"(Level IV)*

If group members are unsure about how empowered they are in relation to a specific topic, it will help to ask:

- *"What level of empowerment is appropriate for this item?"*
- *"What level do you assume you already have?"*
- *"Does the empowerment level need to be negotiated up or down?"*

Adjusting Empowerment Levels

If a group feels that a decision is being made at the wrong level, facilitate a discussion about the empowerment level they think they need. While this is often about gaining more empowerment, there are situations in which groups feel the need to reduce their level of accountability for a decision.

To *raise* empowerment, facilitate a discussion that asks:

- *"What empowerment level is appropriate for this activity?"*
- *"Why does the group need these powers?"*
- *"What are the risks of the group having these powers?"*

Help groups clarify which level is most effective.

- *"What concerns is management likely to have?"*
- *"What checks and balances could be put into place to encourage management to empower you more?"*
- *"What accountabilities are group members prepared to assume individually and as a group to gain more power?"*

Encouraging Groups to Accept Greater Empowerment

There are instances in which group members may feel that they're being asked to assume too much power. This can have a number of root causes:

- there may be a feeling that the actions planned by the group aren't within their job description
- some people are unused to being empowered and are afraid to take risks
- many people may already be overcommitted
- there may be a lack of confidence or skill on the part of some participants
- there may be a lack of true buy-in to the action plans that were created
- there may be a justified lack of trust that the organization is going to support the group's initiatives.

If group members are justified in resisting increased empowerment, you may need to help them make their case. To explore the need to *reduce* empowerment, facilitate a discussion that asks:

- *"What power and authority is appropriate for this activity?"*
- *"Why should the empowerment level be lower?"*
- *"What accountabilities are group members unprepared to assume?"*
- *"What risks should management be made aware of?"*

There are situations, however, in which group members shy away from assuming greater responsibility when they really should take accountability. A common example is in groups where members enjoy analyzying a problem and brainstorming solutions, but back away from taking responsibility for taking action.

Unlike managers, who may have the authority to "order" reluctant employees to take on new tasks, facilitators have to rely on their process skills to encourage people to overcome resistance. If you encounter unjustified resistance to empowerment, use the following line of questioning:

1. **Acknowledge the resistance**—don't ignore or deny it:
   "I can tell by your reaction that you don't want to take on responsibility for this decision/program."

2. **Invite members to verbalize their reticence**—allow them to vent their fears and concerns:
   "Why do you think you shouldn't take on responsibility for this?"

Groups are often reluctant to take on empowerment.

3. Empathize with their situation—sympathize without agreeing:

> *"I can understand that you're concerned about taking on more
> responsibility at this time."*

4. Engage them in identifying strategies—ask them to identify conditions
for overcoming their resistance:

> *"Under what conditions would you consider assuming more responsibility?"*
> *"What assurances, training or support would make you feel you'd be
> willing to give it a try?"*

5. Paraphrase and summarize their statements—encourage them to
agree to greater empowerment by ratifying their suggestions:

> *"So you're saying that you'd be willing to take this on with some
> training and coaching."*

In most situations, group members will identify feasible and realistic things that
can be done to encourage them to buy-in further. If, on the other hand, group
members state unreasonable conditions, like having their pay doubled, don't react.
Record all unreasonable ideas along with the others until the list of conditions
is complete. Then ask the group to help review the list of conditions to identify
which are feasible and which are unrealistic. In most cases, other group members
will edit out the more outrageous demands of their peers.

Does this approach always work? The truth is that nothing works in every
situation. It is, however, the only process tool available given the facilitator's lack
of true power over the group. If this approach fails to work, the facilitator may
have to refer the problem of group reluctance to assume accountability to a
manager, who may order members to take on these new tasks.

Be aware that bringing in the manager to order members to take on more
empowerment is not a very facilitative strategy and will most likely regress the
group's maturity backwards to a dependent state of obedience. Since this is
undesirable to say the least, facilitators are urged to always try a process
approach in the hope that the members will overcome their own barriers.

Shifting Decision-Making Paradigms

You need to be aware that when organizations start using groups to make decisions that were formerly made by managers, this often represents a major shift in
the power arrangements and cultural values of the whole organization.

Many managers are used to listening to input and then making all of the important decisions themselves. Such patterns are a reality that facilitators need to be
aware of. In these situations, staff input into decisions may well represent a major
cultural shift. Sensitivity is needed to help both leaders and members understand
the value of participative decisions, and to create the right setting in which people
can be encouraged to express their ideas freely.

When working with a group you don't know, never assume that participative decision making is understood or practiced by either the group or the leader.

Instead, check by asking questions that probe how the organization normally makes decisions: are member decisions often overturned by leaders, and to what extent are groups empowered to make important decisions?

Leaders who are accustomed to a directive style may have concerns about relinquishing control. These leaders need a side conversation in order to buy into the value of staff participation in decision making. They also need to understand how this power shift opens the door for them to play new roles.

Some points that may be helpful in persuading a leader to respect and accept group decisions include:

- group decision making has the benefit of getting more ideas, building commitment and getting members to take greater responsibility for implementing actions

- "risky" decisions can be handled in such a way that members may simply offer ideas or make recommendations. In these cases, the leader has the final approval of the outcome (empowerment levels II or III)

- decisions that group members are empowered to make without needing final approval can be given clear parameters to insure they meet key success criteria, such as: compliance with budgetary guidelines, support of the overall strategic plan, etc. (empowerment level IV)

- group decision making relieves the leader of many tasks and frees him or her to play more strategic roles in the organization

If the leader remains dubious about participative decision making, you'll need to get clarity about which specific decisions can be made by the group and which can't. The four-level empowerment chart can be used to identify the level of decision-making power members will be given on specific issues.

While facilitators can take part in sessions in which participants are only giving their ideas and have no decision-making powers (level II), it should be made clear that this isn't the full use of any group's powers.

The bottom line is that there has to be total clarity about which decisions can be made by members, and to what extent they'll be given management support for their suggestions. When parameters aren't specifically defined, group decisions are often overturned later on.

Raising empowerment levels and using facilitation creates a paradigm shift.

The Six Decision-Making Options

When groups need to make decisions, there are six distinct decision-making methods available. Each of these options represents a different approach. Each has pros and cons associated with it. The decision option should always be chosen carefully to be sure it's the most appropriate method for the decision that's before the group. These six options are:

Spontaneous Agreement

This happens occasionally when there's a solution that is favored by everyone and 100 percent agreement seems to happen automatically. These types of decisions are usually made quickly and automatically. They are fairly rare and often occur in connection with the more trivial or simple issues.

Pros—it's fast, easy, everyone is happy; it unites the group.

Cons—may be too fast; perhaps the issue actually needed discussion.

Uses—when lack of discussion isn't vital (i.e., issues are trivial); or when issues are not complex, requiring no in-depth discussion.

One Person Decides

This is a decision that the group decides to refer to one person to make on behalf of the group. A common misconception among teams is that every decision needs to be made by the whole group. In fact, a one-person decision is often a faster and more efficient way to get resolution. The quality of any one person's decision can be raised considerably if the person making the decision gets advice and input from other group members before deciding.

Pros—it's fast and accountability is clear. Can result in commitment and buy-in if people feel their ideas are represented.

Cons—it can divide the group if the person deciding doesn't consult, or makes a decision that others can't live with. A one-person decision typically lacks in both the buy-in and synergy that come from a group decision-making process.

Uses—when the issue is unimportant or small; or when there's a clear expert in the group; or when only one person has the information needed to make the decision and can't share it; or when one person is solely accountable for the outcome.

Compromise

A negotiated approach is applicable when there are two or more distinct options and members are strongly polarized (neither side is willing to accept the solution/ position put forth by the other side). A middle position is then created that incorporates ideas from both sides. Throughout the process of negotiation, everyone wins a few favorite points, but also loses a few items he or she liked. The outcome is, therefore, something that no one is totally satisfied with. In compromises, no one feels he or she got what he or she originally wanted, so the emotional reaction is often "It's not really what I wanted, but I'm going to have to live with it."

Be wary of spontaneous agreement for making important decisions.

Many groups ignore the fact that many decisions are best made by one person.

A compromise creates feelings of both win and lose.

Pros—it generates lots of discussion and does create a solution.

Cons—negotiating when people are pushing a favored point of view tends to be adversarial, hence this approach divides the group. In the end, everyone wins, but everyone also loses.

Uses—when two opposing solutions are proposed, neither of which are acceptable to everyone; or when the group is strongly polarized and compromise is the only alternative.

Multi-voting

This is a priority-setting tool that is useful for making decisions when the group has a lengthy set of options and rank ordering the options, based on a set of criteria, will clarify the best course of action. (Refer to page 159.)

Pros—it's systematic, objective, democratic, non-competitive and participative. Everyone wins somewhat, and feelings of loss are minimal. It's a fast way of sorting out a complex set of options. Often feels consensual.

Cons—it's often associated with limited discussion, hence, limited understanding of the options. This may force choices on people that may not be satisfactory to them, because the real priorities do not rise to the surface or people are swayed by each other if the voting is done out in the open, rather than electronically or by ballot.

Uses—when there's a long list of alternatives or items from which to choose to identify the best course of action.

Majority Voting

This involves asking people to choose the option they favor, once clear choices have been identified. Usual methods are a show of hands or secret ballot. The quality of voting is always enhanced if there's good discussion to share ideas before the vote is taken.

Pros—it's fast and decisions can be of higher quality if the vote is preceded by a thorough analysis.

Cons—it can be too fast and low in quality if people vote based on their personal feelings without the benefit of hearing each other's thoughts or facts. It creates winners and losers, hence dividing the group. The show of hands method may put pressure on people to conform.

Uses—when there are two distinct options and one or the other must be chosen; when decisions must be made quickly, and a division in the group is acceptable. When consensus has been attempted and can't be reached.

Consensus Building

Involves everyone clearly understanding the situation or problem to be decided, analyzing all of the relevant facts together, and then jointly developing solutions that represent the whole group's best thinking about the optimal decision. It's characterized by a lot of listening, healthy debate and testing of options. Consensus generates a decision about which everyone says, "I can live with it."

Multi-voting is a good tool if there are a lot of options or a lot of people involved.

The quality of any voting exercise increases dramatically if it's preceded by a thorough discussion.

Pros—it's a collaborative effort that unites the group. It demands high involvement. It's systematic, objective and fact-driven. It builds buy-in and high commitment to the outcome.

Cons—it's time-consuming and produces low-quality decisions if done without proper data collection or if members have poor interpersonal skills.

Uses—when decisions will impact the entire group; when buy-in and ideas from all members are essential; when the importance of the decision being made is worth the time it will take to complete the consensus process properly.

Remember that each option has its place, so choose the most appropriate method before each decision-making session.

Decision Options Chart			
Option	**Pros**	**Cons**	**Uses**
Spontaneous Agreement	• fast, easy • unites	• too fast • lack of discussion	• when full discussion isn't critical • trivial issues
One Person	• can be fast • clear accountability	• lack of input • low buy-in • no synergy	• when one person is the expert • individual willing to take sole responsibility
Compromise	• discussion • creates a solution	• adversarial • win/lose • divides the group	• when positions are polarized; consensus improbable
Multi-voting	• systematic • objective • participative • feels like a win	• limits dialogue • influenced choices • real priorities may not surface	• to sort or prioritize a long list of options
Voting	• fast • high quality with dialogue • clear outcome	• may be too fast • winners and losers • no dialogue • influenced choices	• trivial matter • when there are clear options • if division of group is OK
Consensus Building	• collaborative • systematic • participative • discussion-oriented • encourages commitment	• takes time • requires data and member skills	• important issues • when total buy-in matters

The Importance of Consensus

The crucial importance of creating consensus simply cannot be overstated and must be fully understood by all facilitators. In fact, facilitation and consensus building are based on the same set of core values and beliefs.

Besides being the #1 choice as a decision mode for all important decisions, facilitators are constantly building consensus with everything they do. The following are all examples of consensus activities:

- Summarizing a complex set of ideas to the satisfaction of group members
- Gaining buy-in from all members as to the purpose or goal of a session
- Getting everyone's input into a clear goal and objectives
- Linking thoughts together so people can formulate a common idea
- Making notes on a flip chart in such a way that each member feels they've been heard and is satisfied with what's been recorded

Because all facilitation activities must strive to be collaborative, participative, synergistic and unifying, all facilitation activities are essentially consensus building in nature!

Hallmarks of the Consensus Process

Regardless of whether a structured consensus process is being used to reach a decision, or if the facilitator is informally working to gather group thoughts, the same hallmarks of the consensus process are always present:

- lots of ideas are being shared
- everyone's ideas are heard
- there's active listening and paraphrasing to clarify ideas
- people build on each other's ideas
- no one's trying to push a pre-determined solution; instead, there's an open and objective quest for new options
- the final solution is based on sound information
- when the final solution is reached, people feel satisfied that they were part of the decision
- everyone feels so consulted and involved that even though the final solution isn't the one they would have chosen working on their own, they can readily "live with it."

There are some situations in which the decisions being made are so important that consensus is the only acceptable method to be used. In these cases, the group must agree to keep discussing until everyone indicates that he or she can live with the outcome.

Defaulting to voting (or any other technique that creates division within the group) for important decisions may allow dissenters to absolve themselves of responsibility for important group outcomes.

Consensus building is at the heart of facilitation.

Some decisions are so important that only consensus will do.

If one or two members express reluctance to support a particular decision, facilitators need to use the strategies for overcoming resistance outlined on page 123. This involves openly asking resistors:

1. *"What stops you from supporting this idea?"*
2. *"What changes, amendments, or additions would make this an idea you could live with?"*

One of the major contributions of any facilitator is in helping a group overcome the temptation to "pressure" dissenters into agreement. By openly accepting and discussing differences, facilitators help members reach decisions that have been objectively explored and tested.

Never end a consensus exercise by asking if everyone is happy or if everyone agrees with the outcome. Consensus is not about agreement. A true consensus is a decision that people feel they can accept. At the end of even a great consensus process, people have usually made concessions and are usually not getting everything they wanted.

Consensus isn't designed to make people happy or leave them in 100 percent agreement. Its goal is to create an outcome that represents the best feasible course of action, given the circumstances.

Don't ask *"Do we all agree?"* **OR** *"Is everyone happy?"*

Instead ask *"Have we got a well-thought-through outcome that we can all feel committed to implementing, and that everyone can live with?"*

Things to Watch for in Decision Making

 ___ Be clear up-front on the process to be used. Explain any tools or techniques that will be used.

___ Ask people what assumptions they're operating under, either about the issue or the organizational constraints. Note these and test them with the rest of the group.

___ Conflict is a natural part of many decision-making discussions. Always confront differences assertively and collaboratively. Don't strive to avoid conflict or accommodate by asking people to be nice and get along.

___ Urge people not to fold or just give in if they feel they have important ideas. When everyone agrees just to make things run smoothly, the result is "group think." This creates poor decisions made just to get it over with and insure that everyone stays friends.

___ If the group has chosen to go for consensus because the issue is important, stick with it, even if the going gets tough. Beware of the tendency to start voting, coin tossing and bargaining to make things easier.

___ Be very particular about achieving closure on any items that get decided. Test for consensus and make sure things are final before letting the group move on to other topics.

___ Stop the action if things start "spinning" or behaviors get ineffective. Ask: *"What are we doing well? What aren't we doing so well?"* and *"What do we need to do about it?"* Then act on all suggestions.

Effective Decision-Making Behaviors

To make any decision process work, group members need to behave in specific ways. These behaviors can be suggested to the group or generated as norms in advance of any decision-making session.

Behaviors That Help	Behaviors That Hinder
Listening to others' ideas politely, even when you don't agree	Interrupting people in mid-sentence
Paraphrasing the main points made by another person, especially if you're about to contradict the person's ideas	Not acknowledging the ideas that others have put on the table
Praising others' ideas	Criticizing others' ideas, as opposed to giving them useful feedback
Building on others' ideas	Pushing your own ideas while ignoring others' input
Asking others to critique your ideas, and accepting the feedback	Getting defensive when your ideas are assessed
Being open to accepting alternative courses of action	Sticking only to your ideas and blocking suggestions for alternatives
Dealing with facts	Basing arguments on feelings
Staying calm and friendly toward colleagues	Getting overly emotional; showing hostility in the face of any disagreement

Sharing this sheet may help encourage group effectiveness.

Steps in the Systematic Consensus-Building Process

When an *important* decision needs to be made, the following should take place:

- the matter to be decided is allocated adequate time on the agenda
- members are given ample time to do their homework and gather needed information
- the facilitator helps the group write a clear statement describing the item that needs to be decided
- the assumptions around the decision-making process are discussed: things like empowerment level, budget, timing, role of members, etc.
- the facilitator helps the group identify the desired outcome or goal of the discussion
- the facilitator insures that appropriate norms are in place, especially if the discussion has the potential to become stormy
- the facilitator explains the key steps in the systematic consensus-building process
- the facilitator helps the group conduct a thorough analysis of the current situation; underlying causes are uncovered
- after a thorough analysis of the topic, group members start to generate possible solutions; all ideas are recorded without judgment
- the group then develops a set of criteria and uses them to judge potential solutions
- the final solution is ratified as one that "everyone can live with" and a clear course of action is described to insure follow-through
- to insure follow-through, the team troubleshoots their action plan by anticipating potential stumbling blocks
- roles and responsibilities are specified and a reporting mechanism is designed
- as members leave the meeting, they evaluate the process and the outcome in order to improve future decision-making meetings.

The worksheets on the following pages provide structure for the process outlined above. Refer to the section on *Process Tools* (Chapter 8) for more in-depth descriptions of the various tools mentioned in key steps.

Experienced facilitators will notice that this decision process is a modified version of *Systematic Problem Solving* (Chapter 8). That's because systematic problem solving is a consensual process that provides a solid foundation for any group seeking to resolve important issues. It's the most important tool in the facilitator's repertoire and should be taught to all groups.

Use a systematic process to arrive at collaborative decisions.

Consensus Building Worksheet

Use these steps systematically to provide structure to an important decision-making process:

Step 1. Write a statement that describes the decision that needs to be made:

"What's the item or issue that we'll be deciding?"

_____

_____

_____

_____

_____

Step 2. Discuss the assumptions surrounding the topic:

"How empowered is the group on this topic?"

"What are the budget parameters?"

"What's the timing?"

_____

_____

_____

_____

_____

Step 3. Identify the desired outcome

"What would a high-quality decision look like?"

"How will it change the current situation?"

_____

_____

_____

_____

_____

Step 4. Create appropriate norms for the situation

"What rules do we need to have in place for this conversation?"

"How do we assure that we have a healthy debate instead of a heated argument?"

_____

_____

_____

_____

_____

Step 5. Explain the key steps in the systematic consensus-building process and allocate times for each step.

Process Step   *Time Required*

_____
_____
_____
_____
_____

Total time required = _____

Step 6. Analyze the current situation to uncover underlying elements.

> *"What are all of the relevant facts that describe the current situation?"*
> *"What are the underlying causes of noticeable symptoms?"*

_____
_____
_____
_____
_____

Step 7. Generate potential solutions using brainstorming or written brainstorming.

> *"What are possible solutions given our analysis?"*

_____
_____
_____
_____
_____

Step 8. Evaluate solutions against criteria.

> *"What criteria should we consider to help us sort through all of the possible solutions?"*
> *"Are all of the criteria equal in importance, or do we need to give some greater weight than others?"*

Examples of "criteria" include: *cost, impact, difficulty/ease, timeliness, urgency, match with priorities, customer need, innovative, cost reduction, impact on quality, employee satisfaction, health and safety, environmental impact, etc.*

Step 8. Evaluate solutions against criteria. (cont'd)

Criteria (weight)	Solutions					
	#1	#2	#3	#4	#5	#6
( )						
( )						
( )						
( )						
Totals						

How to rate:

Step 1— rate how critical each criteria item is to the final decision. Use a scale of 1 to 3, where 1 = somewhat important, 2 = important, and 3 = critical

Step 2— rate each solution on how well it meets each criteria item. Use a scale of 1 to 3, where 1 = poorly meets the criteria, 2 = somewhat meets the criteria, 3 = meets criteria very well

Step 3— weight each solution by multiplying the two ratings together (created in *Steps 1 & 2*) for each criteria item. Add all the criteria weights for each solution to determine each solution's total weight

Step 9. Identify the components of the final solution that everyone can live with:

"Which of the potential solutions become part of the action strategy?"
"Can we make a statement that sums up our plan going forward?"

_____

_____

_____

_____

_____

Step 10. Plan for Action

Indicate:

What will be done and how?	By whom?	By when?	Results indicator(s)?

Step 11. Troubleshoot the Action Plan

What are all of the things that can get in the way of implementing our actions?	*What can we do about each of these possible blocks?*

Step 12. Report on Progress

"When will we meet to report back on any progress?"

_____
_____
_____
_____
_____

"How will we report back?" (written, verbal)

_____
_____
_____
_____

"What do we need to report on?"

_____
_____
_____
_____
_____

"Who else in the organization needs to be made aware of our decisions and action steps? How do we communicate with them?"

_____
_____
_____
_____

Step 13. Evaluate the decision process using forcefield analysis or the decision process survey on page 106.

What was effective about today's decision process? What worked well?	What was ineffective about today's decision process? What didn't work well?

Symptoms, Causes and Cures of Poor Decisions

When groups make poor-quality decisions, one or more of the following symptoms may be in evidence:

Symptom #1: Aimless drifting and random discussions.

The same topic gets kicked around meeting after meeting without resolution. Feels like the group is spinning its wheels.

Cause: No plan or process for approaching the decision.

Group members simply launch into the discussion without any thought to which tools to use. Without a systematic approach, people start proposing solutions before there has been a thorough analysis of the situation. There is a lack of proper information. Everyone puts his or her favorite solution on the table. No one takes notes. No solution is ever definitively agreed to. Detailed action plans aren't written down.

Cure: The group needs a structured approach to decision making that uses the right decision-making tool and is assertively facilitated.

Symptom #2: The group uses voting on important items where total buy-in is important, then uses consensus to decide trivial issues.

Cause: A lack of understanding of decision-making options.

The group doesn't understand the six key decision-making options and when to use each of them.

Cure: The group needs to become familiar with the six main decision-making options and consciously decide which to use before launching into any decision-making discussion.

Symptom #3: The group always seems to run out of time just when the important decisions get onto the table.

Cause: Poor time management.

Time isn't budgeted or monitored. There's no detailed agenda that sets aside sufficient time to deal with important items. Hence, time is wasted discussing less important aspects. Meetings often start late or run over.

Cure: The group needs to create a detailed agenda before each meeting. During discussions, the facilitator needs to be assertive about keeping the group on track and on time.

Symptom #4: **When an important item is on the table, people get heated and argumentative. No one really listens to the opposing viewpoints. Everyone pushes his or her point in an attempt to "win". Some members dominate, unconcerned that others are silent.**

Cause: Poorly developed group interaction skills.

People have become positional and competitive. No one is listening to the points other people are making, just pushing their own. Facilitation is nonexistent or weak. As a result, there's an absence of the synergy you get when people build on each other's ideas. This confrontational style strains relationships, which only makes things worse.

Cure: The members need training in group effectiveness skills so that they can exhibit more listening, supporting and idea building. If a facilitator is present, he or she should stop the conversation and explain active listening and paraphrasing. When conversation resumes, the facilitator should assure that people are acknowledging each other's points.

Symptom #5: **After a lengthy discussion, it becomes clear that everyone is operating on slightly different assumptions about what the problem is and what the constraints or possibilities are.**

Cause: Failure to check assumptions.

Everyone has a different view of the situation and is basing his or her input on that view. Assumptions are never put on the table for sharing or testing.

Cure: Use probing questions to uncover the assumptions underlying statements made by the members. These questions can be related to the situation, the organization or the people involved. Once assumptions are clarified and validated, members will be operating in the same framework.

Symptom #6: **In spite of the fact that the discussion has been going in circles for some time, no one takes action to get things back on track.**

Cause: No process checking.

Even when things are going nowhere and frustration levels are running high, no one knows to call time-out to take stock and regroup. This, once again, reflects the absence of facilitation.

Cure: Stopping the discussion periodically to ask how things are going, whether the pace is right, whether people feel progress is being made, whether people feel the right approach is being taken. (Refer to the discussion of process checking on page 45.)

Decision Process Survey

Anonymously provide your feedback about your team's decision process.

I. How thoroughly did people do their homework?

1	2	3	4	5
Poor	Fair	Satisfactory	Good	Excellent

2. Was there clarity about their assumptions surrounding the topic?

1	2	3	4	5
Poor	Fair	Satisfactory	Good	Excellent

3. How clear was the goal of the decision process?

1	2	3	4	5
Poor	Fair	Satisfactory	Good	Excellent

4. Did we exhibit effective behaviors in dealing with contentious items?

1	2	3	4	5
Poor	Fair	Satisfactory	Good	Excellent

5. How thorough was our analysis of the current situation?

1	2	3	4	5
Poor	Fair	Satisfactory	Good	Excellent

6. How creative and innovative were the ideas that we generated?

1	2	3	4	5
Poor	Fair	Satisfactory	Good	Excellent

7. How objective and balanced was our evaluation of options?

1	2	3	4	5
Poor	Fair	Satisfactory	Good	Excellent

8. How satisfied are you that the final solution was one that everyone can live with?

1	2	3	4	5
Poor	Fair	Satisfactory	Good	Excellent

9. Were the potential blocks and barriers to action adequately anticipated?

1	2	3	4	5
Poor	Fair	Satisfactory	Good	Excellent

10. Rate your overall assessment of the quality of the decision process.

1	2	3	4	5
Poor	Fair	Satisfactory	Good	Excellent

What would you do to improve our next decision-making session?

_____

_____

Chapter 6
Facilitating Conflict

Dealing with conflict is a fact of every facilitator's life. Consider the following scenario: Imagine yourself facilitating an important meeting. Everything is going along great until you hit agenda item #3. Suddenly two members start arguing. Listening goes out the window, as each person pushes his or her ideas. The rest of the group gets uncomfortable, as the two combatants become more and more emotional. The discussion spins in circles and people get upset!

What do you do now? For starters remember that conflict is often the symptom of a problem with the task or the process. Refer to the strategies for dealing with storming described on page 57 of Chapter Three.

Comparing Arguments and Debates

All facilitators need to be attuned to the differences between a debate and an argument. Healthy debate is essential. If a group doesn't express differences of opinion, then it's basically incapable of making effective decisions. Dysfunctional arguments, on the other hand, lead to disaster. Facilitators don't want to limit debate, they just want to make sure it doesn't become dysfunctional.

Differences of opinion are not only inevitable, but vital for making good decisions.

In Healthy Debates	In Dysfunctional Arguments
↪ people are open to hearing others' ideas	↪ people assume they're right
↪ people listen and respond to ideas even if they don't agree with them	↪ people wait until others have finished talking, then state their ideas without responding to ideas of the other person
↪ everyone tries to understand the views of the other person	↪ no one is interested in how the other person sees the situation
↪ people stay objective and focus on the facts	↪ people get personally attacked and blamed
↪ there's a systematic approach to analyzing the situation and looking for solutions	↪ hot topics get thrashed

It's your approach that will determine whether people debate or argue.

Techniques That Create Healthy Debate	Techniques That Allow Dysfunctional Arguments
→ stay totally neutral → point out differences so they can be understood → insist that people listen politely—have rules and use them → make people paraphrase each other's ideas → ask for concerns → make people focus on facts → problem solve concerns → invite and face feedback → facilitate assertively → get closure and move on	→ join the argument → ignore differences—just pray that they will go away → let people be rude—set no norms → ignore the fact that no one is really hearing anyone else → sidestep hot issues → let people get personal → get defensive → squash dissent → stand by passively → let it drag on and on

Steps in Managing Conflict

When facilitating conflict, divide your strategies into two categories that mirror the steps in conflict management.

Step 1: Venting—This involves listening to people so that they feel heard and so that any built-up emotions are diffused. People are rarely ready to move on to solutions until emotional blocks have been removed.

Step 2: Resolving the issue—Choosing the right structured approach to get to solutions. This can be a collaborative problem-solving activity, compromising, accommodating or consciously avoiding.

Let's examine each step in more detail.

Step 1: Venting People's Emotions

People won't move forward to resolve a problem until their feelings have been vented.

Facilitators need to vent emotions when the following are in evidence:

- people pushing their points of view without being at all receptive to the ideas of others
- people becoming angry, defensive and personal with each other
- negative body language, like glaring and finger pointing
- sarcastic or dismissive remarks
- people "yeah, butting" and criticizing each other's ideas
- quiet people "shutting down" to stay out of it
- extreme anger to the point where relationships are damaged

When negative emotions are in evidence, facilitators need to act quickly so that these emotions don't poison the dynamics of the group. To vent conflict:

- **Slow things down**—get the attention of the group by stopping the action and asking people to slow down. You can use the excuse that you can't take notes as quickly as people are talking. Ask them to start over and repeat key ideas.

- **Stay totally neutral**—never take sides or allow your body language to hint that you favor one idea or one person over another.

- **Stay calm**—maintain your composure and do not raise your own voice. Speak slowly with an even tone. Avoid using emotional body language.

- **Revisit the norms**—point out the existing norms and remind people of their prior agreements. Engage the group in writing new norms.

- **Be assertive**—move into the referee mode. Insist that people speak one at a time. Make them put their hands up and stop people who interrupt others. Don't stand by passively while people fight.

- **Raise awareness**—on a clean sheet of flip chart paper record member ideas about the difference between a debate versus an argument. Ask them which one they want to have.

- **Make interventions**—don't ignore ineffective or dysfunctional behaviors. Refer to page 120 in this chapter for the appropriate wording for making interventions that redirect behavior.

- **Emphasize listening**—paraphrase key points and ask others to do the same thing. Hand out, discuss and encourage the practices outlined on page 110.

- **Do a process check**—stop the action any time emotions get out of hand or if the discussion is spinning in circles. Intervene by saying:

  > *"I'm noticing that points are being made with considerable emotion. What can we do to change the tone to create a healthy debate?"*

- **Use a structured approach**—use techniques such as force-field analysis, multi-voting, systematic problem solving, cause and effect analysis, etc., to interject needed objectivity. Don't let any discussion rage on without imposing structure and systematically capturing key ideas. Chapter 8 provides detailed descriptions of many useful process tools.

- **Use the flip chart**—make note of key points so they aren't lost and to prevent group members from repeating points. Read back flip chart notes whenever you want to regain control.

- **Create closure**—make sure that the debating is really going somewhere. Ask group members to help summarize what has been agreed. Test these items for agreement. Help the group create action plans to insure implementation of key suggestions.

In conflicts you need to facilitate calmly yet assertively!

Listen-Empathize-Clarify-Seek Permission-Resolve

1. Listen—Instead of arguing when you hear a point you disagree with, listen attentively to the other person's main points. Let people share their views without interruption. Look interested and say things like:

> *"Tell me more. That's interesting. Uh-huh."*
> *"I'm not sure I understand. Could you go over that again?"*

2. Empathize—Accept the views of the other person even if you don't agree with them. Let people know you understand their feelings. Say:

> *"I don't blame you for feeling that way. I see what you mean."*
> *"I understand how you feel. I'm sure I'd feel the same way if…."*

3. Clarify—Delve deeper to insure that you have a clear understanding of what the other person is saying to you. Say:

> *"Let me see if I've got it straight; what you're saying is…."*
> *"Is it possible that…. The idea you're proposing is…."*

4. Seek Permission—Tell your side after the other person has expressed all of his or her concerns and feels clearly understood. Say:

> *"Now that I understand your views, can I explain mine?"*
> *"It seems that this would be a good time to bring up a few points you haven't mentioned."*

5. Resolve the Issue—Once you have both heard each other, this is the time to start dealing with the problem together.

Step 2: Resolving Issues

Here are five basic approaches you can choose from, once emotions have been vented, in order to resolve the underlying issue:

Avoid ignore the conflict in the hope that it will go away. Maintain silence or try to change the subject.

Accommodate ask people to be more tolerant and accept each other's views. Ask them to try getting along. This sometimes involves asking one person to give in to another person.

Compromise look for the middle ground between highly polarized views. Ask each person to give up some of what he or she wants, in order to get other items he or she thinks are more important.

Compete use force to make points and quell any conflicts. Go for a personal win even if the other person feels like he or she has lost the argument.

Collaborate face the conflict, draw people's attention to it, surface the issues and resolve them in a win/win way by using a systematic problem solving approach.

Use this handout if people need reminders about how to act.

The Five Conflict Options: Pros and Cons

Each of the aforementioned approaches can work in specific situations. Facilitators need to understand each one and choose the one that suits the situation.

Avoiding—When conflict is avoided, nothing gets resolved. Yet this is the right approach to use if the issue at stake is very trivial, can't be solved or will result in a total lose/lose situation for the group. Avoiding is sometimes a wise interim strategy to give people a chance to calm down before addressing issues.

When people are in conflict, avoiding can be a wise interim strategy.

The main consequence of avoiding is that issues aren't resolved and there's no creativity applied towards finding a solution. The problem remains to fester and can crop up later. While avoiding has its place, groups become ineffective if they avoid too many issues.

Accommodating—This is a social response aimed more at keeping the peace than solving the problem. This approach can involve asking everyone to just get along or asking one party in a conflict to give in to the other party.

In some conflict situations, one party ought to be encouraged to think about giving in.

Accommodating is the appropriate approach in situations in which one person is only slightly interested in the issue, while the other party cares deeply. It's also the right approach to take when exploration of the issue reveals that one party is wrong. This style is most applicable to family and other social gatherings in which tolerance and civility may be of greater importance than finding the right answer.

The consequence of accommodating is that the underlying issues are often left unexplored in the interest of keeping the peace.

Compromising—This is a mediated approach to managing conflict that is used when two people or two groups have formulated strong positions. Neither party feels he or she can accept the position of the other, so a neutral middle option needs to be developed.

Compromising is adversarial and can leave people divided.

The good thing about compromising is that it does yield a solution. The problem is that both parties must give up points to get others. The process of compromise also tends to be adversarial. People push their views in the hope that their position prevails.

At the end of a compromise, people feel that they've both won and lost. They may also harbor negative feelings towards the other party because of the adversarial nature of the process. Compromise leaves people feeling, "I'm going to have to live with it!"

Competing—This is a strategy of defending oneself and arguing one's point of view in order to score a win over another person. Competing is a contest of wills in which the person who wins does so at the expense of the other person.

Competing is a combative and hence unacceptable approach.

Competing has its place in those situations that are clearly defined as competitive, such as sports and war. In these situations, the winner doesn't worry about the feelings of the loser. Since competing is combative and adversarial, facilitators never use this approach to settle issues.

Collaborating—This approach strives to build consensus. It involves naming the issue and then engaging group members in analyzing the facts of the current situation, generating creative ideas, objectively sorting through potential solutions and agreeing on a course of action.

Collaborating relies on objective information. Everyone inputs ideas. People are encouraged to listen and build on each other's points. Solutions are generated through the use of non-competitive processes such as brainstorming. The best course of action is determined by applying a set of criteria to the choices available.

At the end of a collaboration, everyone feels that he or she was heard and that the final strategy reflects his or her thinking. While the final outcome may not be exactly what they would have decided on their own, all members feel that they have had a say. Because collaboration emphasizes working together for a win/win, it creates a consensus. At the end of a conflict resolved through collaboration, people's feelings about the solution are: "I can live with it!"

The main drawback to collaboration is that it requires a great deal of time and thus may result in a waste of energy if used on an insignificant issue.

The Five Options in Action

Consider the following conflict situation:

Fred and Bill are getting very heated talking about whether or not to conduct classroom computer training for the new software about to be introduced in the department.

Fred thinks that hands-on help, while people work with the system, is the way to go. He thinks the proposed two days of classroom time is costly and takes people off the job for too long.

Bill is arguing that the new system is too complex for people to learn on the job and that too many mistakes will be made if people learn through trial and error.

Now consider possible facilitator responses using each of the five conflict options. Which work? Which don't? Why?

The facilitator uses avoidance
"You two seem quite deadlocked. Let's move on and discuss something else within our remaining time."

The facilitator encourages accommodation
"Look Bill, Fred is pretty adamant that his people not be off the job for any length of time. Since most of the staff are in his department, could you forget the idea of training classes?"

The facilitator fosters competing
"You both have strong arguments that you think are right."

The facilitator suggests a compromise
"Is there a middle ground, an option that combines both approaches?"

The facilitator uses a collaborative technique

"Let's put all of the facts of the situation on the table. What are the details of our work and time pressures? Which skills do people need? What are all the possible options for getting people trained? What are the characteristics of the best options? Which of our options looks like it meets those criteria? What is the best course of action?"

In the above five scenarios you will have noticed:

Avoiding doesn't deal with the issue	⇢ Use it in those 10% of situations when issues can't be resolved
Accommodating just smoothes things over	⇢ Use it only in those 5% of situations when keeping the peace is of more importance than finding a solution
Competing divides groups and creates win/lose	⇢ Facilitators should never let people compete! 0% applicability
Compromise seeks to find the middle ground	⇢ Use it in those 20% of situations when faced with polarized choices
Collaboration gets people working together to find the best solution for everyone	⇢ This is the #1 preferred approach for all facilitators. Use it in 65% of all conflict situations

Collaboration encourages people to work together to objectively seek solutions that they can all live with. Because it's consensual, it unites and generates solutions that everyone feels committed to implementing. It's the superior conflict option!

Assumptions underlying collaboration:

Collaboration is a superior way of solving a problem during a meeting; however, a number of conditions need to be in place to insure a successful outcome. Members must:

 __ have sufficient trust among themselves to open up and be supportive of each other when necessary

     __ have a positive intent to work towards a win/win solution

     __ have relevant information on hand to make a sound decision

     __ have the time to make this decision

     __ believe the topic is important enough to warrant spending the time it will take

Collaboration is the optimal approach for settling disputes.

Conflict Management Norms

Anytime you anticipate that a session has the potential to become contentious or if the group has had stormy meetings in the past, it's important to create new norms specially targeted for conflict situations. As with all other norms, these are created by the members, preferably at the start of the session. Use the following questions to trigger the discussion:

> *"What behaviors and rules should we adhere to if we find ourselves getting into serious disagreements?"*
>
> *"What can we do to insure that we have a healthy debate instead of a heated argument?"*

Some sample norms targeted at conflict situations include:

* we'll speak one at a time
* we'll look at each other when we speak and acknowledge any valid points made by the other person
* we'll accept all ideas as valid when presented
* we'll build on each other's ideas
* we won't dismiss any idea without really exploring it
* we'll make sure everyone is heard—not just a few people
* we won't get emotional, argumentative or personal
* no one will attack anyone else
* if the discussion gets heated or we start going in circles, we'll call a time-out and look at how we are doing things
* no one will deliberately block the group from reaching a final solution by taking a position
* we'll take a systematic approach to resolving issues rather than just pushing personal points of view

Once conflict norms have been established, refer to them at strategic moments to encourage effective behaviors. You can also use the conflict norms in the middle of a session as a mid-point check.

Norms are your best tool for heading off potential conflict.

Giving and Receiving Feedback

Every facilitator encounters situations that require feedback: perhaps the meeting is dragging or maybe people are exhausted and need a break; perhaps the group needs to improve its interpersonal behaviors. Managing feedback is an important facilitator responsibility. Feedback involves stopping the group's discussions to ask them to assess how it's going. Feedback can be about:

- how the meeting is going
- whether or not the goal is being achieved
- how members are conducting themselves
- how decisions are being made
- how the facilitator is doing

General Principles of Good Feedback

Feedback is always meant to be positive. Its goal is to improve the current situation or performance—its goal is never to criticize or offend. The structure of giving feedback is a reflection of this positive intent. No matter what form feedback takes, the following general principles always apply:

Be descriptive rather than evaluative—tell the other person what you notice or what has happened. Avoid all comments about him or her as a person.

Be specific instead of general—describe exactly what happened so that facts, not impressions, form the basis of the feedback.

Solicit feedback rather than impose it—ask the other person if you can give him or her feedback. If the person says no, respect that this may not be a good time. Collaborate to determine a more convenient time.

Time it—feedback should be given as soon as possible after the situation being described.

Focus on what can be changed—make suggestions for improvements that the person is capable of implementing.

Check the feedback—make sure your understanding is accurate and fair. Check with the person, or even with others, to avoid misjudging the situation.

Demonstrate caring—offer feedback with the positive intent of helping the other person.

Feedback Formats

Feedback can take a number of forms. You'll find sample formats throughout this book, but here are a few to get you started. You can:

- Hand out a survey for members to complete at a break. Then share results with the group for their analysis and action planning.
- Post selected questions on a flip chart. Ask members to rate each item.
- Discuss the results and look for solutions to any items that received low ratings.

• Ask group members to give each other written feedback in response to questions such as: "What things are you doing well?" and/or, "What could you do to become even more effective?"
• Use Force-field Analysis (see Chapter 8, page 161) to discuss what is and is not going well. The group then creates remedies for all of the things that aren't going well.
• Simply ask members to tell you what you could do better.

The Eight-Step Feedback Process

Every facilitator needs to know the core model for giving feedback.

Imagine you're at a meeting at which no one is putting the real issues on the table. Everyone is being polite and the problems of the group aren't being resolved. In this situation, the facilitator needs to stop the action and give feedback so the participants can resolve their problems and move on. It's never easy giving direct feedback, so use the right language and follow the steps outlined below:

Step 1: Ask permission to offer feedback

Asking permission lets people tell you if this is a bad time to hear feedback, and insures that they're ready to pay careful attention. Asking permission is a way of signaling that you intend to give feedback.

"I'm going to stop this meeting now and give you some input that I think you need to hear. Is that OK?"

Step 2: Describe specifically what you are observing

Give a clear and specific description of what you observed. Avoid generalizing, exaggerating or offering emotional accounts.

"During the interviews I held with more than half of you, the issue of some people not pulling their weight was mentioned by everyone as the most serious problem facing this team. We have been talking about team problems for two hours and yet no one has mentioned this issue."

Step 3: Tell them about the direct impact of their actions

Describe the impact on individuals, the program or the department. Keep it very objective and don't get personal. Avoid blaming. Deal with the facts of the current situation.

"Since the issue of people not pulling their weight has not been mentioned, there's a good chance that these discussions are not going to resolve your most serious team problem."

Step 4: Give the other person(s) an opportunity to explain

Listen actively, using attentive body language and paraphrasing key points.

"You're telling me that this problem isn't being discussed because it's too sensitive and people are concerned about offending each other."

Step 5: Draw out ideas from the others

Frame the whole thing as a problem to be solved. Get people to offer their ideas. Remember that people are most likely to implement their own ideas. The more they self-prescribe, the better. Support their efforts at self-correction.

> *"What do you think we could do to make it feel safe enough so that*
> *this issue can be discussed? What guidelines will create the comfort we need?"*

Step 6: Offer specific suggestions for improvement

Make suggestions that will improve the situation. Wherever possible, build on the ideas suggested by others.

> *"I think the guidelines you have come up with are excellent. I'd like to*
> *add a few ideas about how we can tackle this with sensitivity.*
> *Would this be OK?"*

Step 7: Summarize and express your support

Demoralizing people does not set the stage for improved performance while offering encouragement and ending on an optimistic note does.

> *"I want to thank you for being willing to tackle this tough subject."*

Step 8: Follow up

Make sure you end the feedback discussion with clear action steps. This insures that the whole exercise doesn't need to be repeated later on.

> *"I'm going to stop the action in about an hour and check with you to see if we're*
> *now tackling our real problems and if the guidelines we set are working."*

The Language of Feedback

Here are a few more examples about language you can add to your tool kit to enhance the effectiveness of your feedback.

Openers to feedback:

> *"I'd like to give you input about ..."*
> *"I have a concern about ..."*
> *"I have information that I think you might be interested in."*
> *"I'd like to make a suggestion, if you're interested."*

Examples of feedback statements:

> *"Instead of (telling me what you think I should do), it would be better if you would*
> *(ask for my opinion)."*
> *"I know that you have a lot on your plate but I need (your full attention now)."*
> *"When you (keep on looking at your watch), I sense that you are/are not*
> *(getting any value out of this discussion)."*
> *"I'd like to propose that we try (openly discussing any problems) rather than*
> *trying to (keep them to ourselves)."*

Facilitators use specific language to share their observations.

Avoid "usually" or "always," as these words may offer more emphasis than you intended, or evoke a negative reaction. Never use assumptive labels that describe personal traits, such as "lazy," "thoughtless" and "sloppy." Instead, offer specific details about what the person did and when. Try to choose "how about," "let's try" or "would you consider?" in place of "should."

Tips for Receiving Feedback

If you've ever been involved in a feedback exercise, you know how difficult it can be—especially if you're on the receiving end. To make it easier for the giver, teach participants how to receive feedback in a non-defensive manner. Share the following tips:

Always encourage people to be open and non-defensive.

Listen actively
Make eye contact with the speaker. Ask probing questions to make sure you understand what's being said.

Don't get emotional
Breathe deeply. Sit back. Adopt a relaxed body posture. Lower your voice. Speak slowly.

Don't get defensive
This isn't aimed at you personally. Understand the other person's perspective before presenting your side of the story. Ask for more details on points you don't agree with.

Accept the input
Even when you don't agree with all of it, there will be some good ideas – accept these. This shows respect for the other person's perspective.

Work to improve
Devote your energy to finding improvements rather than disputing observations. Do not put all of the burden for finding solutions on the other person. Offer ideas of your own.

Making Interventions

During any workshop or meeting, there may be occasions when the facilitator will need to make an intervention. The definition of "intervention" is, "any action or set of actions deliberately taken to improve the functioning of the group." This may be necessary in situations in which:

- two people are having a side conversation
- people are interrupting and not hearing each other's points
- people become inappropriately emotional
- the discussion is stuck or off track

Intervening is like holding up a mirror to the participants so that they can see what they're doing and take steps to correct the problem.

Regardless of its length and complexity, an intervention is always an interruption. You're stopping the discussion about the task to draw member attention to an aspect of the process. Since this constitutes an interruption in the flow of discussion, the aim is always to resolve the problem as quickly as possible so that members can return to their task.

The need to intervene may arise because of one individual, or it may be interpersonal, involving a conflict between two or more people.

Groups can also experience problems that involve all of the members, such as poor listening, or a problem that stems from using the wrong process, for example, using a force-field analysis instead of cause and effect analysis.

You always need to be cautious about whether or not to intervene. If you intervened every single time there was a problem, you would be interrupting too frequently. Instead, keep a watchful eye for repetitive, inappropriate behaviors that aren't resolving themselves.

Interventions are needed in a wide variety of situations.

Deciding Whether or Not to Intervene

Below are questions to ask when deciding if an intervention is advisable:

__ Is the problem serious?
__ Might it go away by itself?
__ How much time will intervening take? Do we have that time?
__ How much of a disruption will intervening cause?
__ How will it impact relationships, the flow of the meeting?
__ Can the intervention hurt the climate or damage anyone's self-esteem?
__ What's the chance that the intervention will work or fail?
__ Do I know these people well enough to do this?
__ Do I have enough credibility to do this?
__ Is it appropriate given their level of openness and trust?

Finally, ask yourself, what will happen if you do nothing? If the answer is that the group will be less effective, you're obligated to take action.

Failing to make an intervention when one is needed makes the facilitator look weak.

Intervention Wording

Interventions are always risky because they can make the situation worse. For this reason, interventions need to be carefully worded. There are generally three distinct components to an intervention statement:

"I'm noticing..."

"I'm concerned ..."

"Would you please ..."

Statement 1: *Describe what you see*—this is non-judgmental and doesn't attribute motive. It's based solely on observations of actual events, i.e., *"I'm noticing that we're now on a topic that's not on our agenda."*

Statement 2: *Make an impact statement.* Tell members how their actions are impacting you, the process or other people. Base this on actual observations, i.e., *"I'm concerned that we aren't going to have time for our other topics."*

Statement 3: *Redirect inneffective behavior(s)*—this can be done by:

(a) *asking* members for their suggestions:
   i.e. *"What do we need to do to get back to our agenda?"*
(b) *telling* members what to do:
   i.e. *"Would you please end this conversation so we can get back on track?"*

Statement 1: Takes a snapshot to create awareness of an ineffective situation. Statement 1 does not resolve the situation.

Statement 2: The impact statements can be omitted from an intervention if they seem to lay excessive guilt on the offending parties. Use your judgment to determine whether or not the situation requires a focus on "impact." A good rule of thumb is to use impact statements when the ineffective behavior is persistent or repetitive and previous interventions have been ignored. Statement 2 does not resolve the situation.

Statement 3: Redirects the situation and is the most important element in an intervention. Statement 3 resolves the situation.

Choose the right language to intervene: don't assume or judge!

Telling Versus Asking

In some interventions, the facilitator tells people what to do, while in others they are asked. When making an intervention, remember the following rules:

- asking is always better than telling because people are more likely to accept their own intervention
- it's always appropriate for facilitators to suggest or tell people what to do on matters of process
- a directive or telling response is appropriate if the individuals are exhibiting extremely dysfunctional behavior or low maturity behavior
- the more a group acts maturely and responsibly, the more effective it is to ask, rather than tell

Intervention Wording for Specific Situations

If group members exhibit behaviors that interfere with progress or cause stress, there are specific responses you can use. You will notice that none of these redirecting statements puts people down or is in any way critical. All of them are tactfully worded to sound supportive of the offending person rather than punitive. Don't be overwhelmed by verbal interventions; realize that the same ten to twenty common scenarios are likely to repeat. What you need to do is anticipate these instances and memorize the appropriate intervention response.

When one person *dominates* the discussion:

> "Al, I'm noticing that we've heard quite a lot from you. I'm concerned that we may not get to hear from others. Please hold the rest of your comments until the end so that other people can be heard."

When two people are *arguing* and not listening to each other:

> "I'm noticing that you are each repeating your points. I'm concerned that you're not hearing each others' excellent ideas. I'm going to ask you both to first paraphrase what the other has said before you make your own comment."

Members are *disregarding* their previously set *norms*:

> "I'm noticing that you're ignoring several of our norms. So let's stop and look back at the norms we set last week. What do we need to do to insure they're being followed?

When the meeting has *totally digressed*:

> "I'd like to point out that we have now digressed and are onto another topic. Is this the topic the team wants to discuss or should we park it and go back to the original agenda item?"

When someone is being *sarcastic*:

> "Ellen, I'm afraid your good ideas aren't being heard because of the tone of voice you're using. How about stating that again, only in a more neutral way?"

When one person is *putting down* the ideas of another:

> "Joe, you have been 'yeah butting' every suggestion Carol has put on the table. I'm going to ask you to tell us the pros and cons of each of these ideas. I want to make sure Carol feels like she's being heard."

When someone has hurled a *personal slur* at someone else:

> "Jim, rather than characterizing Sally as being 'sloppy,' please tell her specifically about the state of the meeting room after her session, so that she can address the situation."

Make your intervention sound and feel supportive of the offenders.

When two people are *discounting* each other's ideas without giving them a fair hearing:

> *"I'm noticing that you're discounting each other's ideas rather quickly. I'm concerned that you're not giving each other's ideas a fair hearing. Please give a quick recap of what the other person said before stating your points."*

When a person makes only *negative remarks* about the ideas of another person:

> *"Mary, I'm noticing that you have a very firm grasp of the downside of Chuck's proposal. I'm concerned that your review lacks balance. Please tell us what the positive aspects are of Chuck's idea."*

When people *run in and out* of a meeting:

> *"In the last ten minutes I've noticed several people going in and out of this meeting. I'm concerned that this is disrupting the discussion. What ought to be done about this?"*

When everyone has *fallen silent*:

> *"I'm noticing that I haven't written any new ideas on the flip chart for quite a while. I'm concerned we may be stalled. What can we do to get things going again?"*

When people display *overt body language* rather than say what they think:

> *"I see you tapping your fingers and rolling your eyes. Tell us what that means . . . are we going too slow? Are we missing major points?"*

When the whole group *looks exhausted*:

> *"I'm noticing that people are slumped in their seats and that we're not making much progress. Tell me what this means. What do we do about it?"*

Dealing with Resistance

As a facilitator, you always need to have a strategy for dealing with situations in which a group resists. Groups can resist your facilitation efforts for a number of reasons:

- the timing or location of the meeting might be poor
- the topic of the meeting may not reflect their needs
- participants may have received insufficient notice of the meeting
- people may be reluctant to take on additional work
- they may suspect that nothing will happen as a result of the meeting
- they may fear that the organization won't support their ideas

Always be on the alert for signs of resistance.

Sometimes this resistance comes out into the open when an outspoken member gets up and vents a concern. At other times it remains hidden, only expressed in people's negative body language or lack of participation.

When you encounter resistance, there's a right and a wrong way to deal with it. Using the wrong way will make the resistance grow. Choosing the right approach will make it manageable.

Resistance Scenarios Exercise

To help you become attuned to dealing with resistance, read the following scenarios and see whether you can figure out what makes one response better than the other:

Resistance Scenario #1
Someone says:

> "The last time we had a two-day retreat nothing happened afterwards. All the promises made were forgotten. People's projects went unsupported. These things are a waste of time!"

Wrong thing to say:

> "Well, we're here now and you've each been handpicked to do this project. Senior management is expecting you to do this. You have to accept that organizations are tough places to get things done. This is no time to turn back."

Right approach for handling resistance:

> A. "Explain why you feel that way. What happened in the past? How did it impact you?"
>
> B. "What would make you a willing participant this time? Under what circumstances or with what assurances will you consider taking up this challenge?"

Assertively making interventions does not violate facilitator neutrality since behavior is a process element.

Resistance Scenario #2

Someone says:

> *"This meeting is a waste of time. We all have tons of work to do back at the office. I suggest we adjourn right now!"*

Wrong thing to say:

> *"We're here now and some good progress has already been made. We booked the room. It will take months for all of us to coordinate our schedules again. We've even ordered lunch!"*

Right approach for handling resistance:

> A. *"I want to hear why you think this meeting is a waste of time. What's gone on so far that's caused this frustration?"*
>
> B. *"What changes can we make to the day to eliminate your main concerns? Under which circumstances would you consider staying?"*

Resistance Scenario #3

Someone says to you:

> *"Nothing personal, but we don't know you. What makes you think you can run this meeting?"*

Wrong thing to say:

> *"I have a Master's degree in Organization Development, and this is exactly the sort of work I've been doing for ten years. Besides, I've been hired by the director of this division to run this meeting."*

Right approach for handling resistance:

> A. *"I can understand that you might have reservations about my role today, since you don't know me. Can you elaborate a bit on what those specific concerns might be?"*
>
> B. *"I want to be an effective facilitator at this meeting. Can you tell me what would make you leave here saying that I had made a valuable contribution?"*

Note: Some interventions are aimed at one person, some at two people, others at the whole group. Resist the temptation to address the whole group if you really should be speaking to one or two people.

If an intervention is too sensitive to make in front of the whole group, by all means offer feedback in private. When doing so, however, you should still use the three-part intervention formula.

The Right Approach for Dealing with Resistance

The right approach for handling resistance always consists of two steps:

Step #1. Invite the resistor to express his or her resistance while you listen actively, paraphrase and offer empathy. Stay calm and act totally supportive of the resistor. Say things like:

> *"Tell me why you feel this way."*
> *"What happened last time?"*
> *"Describe your reluctance."*

Step #2: After all the concerns have been acknowledged, ask questions to prompt the resistor to suggest solutions to the barriers. Make this questioning detailed and complex so that they have to stop and think. Ask things like:

> *"What circumstances would make you willing to stay?"*
> *"What assurance will eliminate your concerns?"*
> *"What supports will enable you to continue?"*

Why This Approach Works

Taking a facilitative or questioning approach works because the resistor is allowed to vent his or her frustration and be heard. The person is then consulted about what to do next. Since people don't generally refuse to act on their own suggestions, most people will abandon their resistance and move forward.

Using the "wrong" approach doesn't work because it's a defensive response. You are basically telling people they have to comply. This stance usually makes people more angry and heightens their resistance.

Every day, meeting leaders handle resistance incorrectly by telling people they have no choice and to "just get on with it." The problem with using this kind of force to blast through resistance is that it erodes people's commitment. They'll comply, but they won't give it their best effort or most creative ideas. That's why choosing the facilitative "ask approach" is always superior to the directive "tell style" when dealing with resistance. Another important reason for using the "ask" approach is that facilitators don't usually have power and control over the groups they're leading. When you have no control over people, ordering them to do something they don't want to do usually doesn't work.

Remember: never get defensive. When you are defenseless you are invincible!

Common Conflict Dilemmas

Regardless of how well a session is prepared, there are always things that can go wrong. The following are common facilitation dilemmas and strategies that can help.

Scenario #1: The group resists being facilitated

The group desperately needs structure for its discussions, but doesn't like following a step-by-step process. They insist they don't want a facilitator. Members say it feels too formal. Sometimes there's a controlling chairperson present and he or she rejects the idea of having a formal facilitator.

Strategy: Offer to facilitate. If rejected, don't hesitate to offer the group methods for tackling the discussion. Facilitate informally: monitor time, ask questions, paraphrase and synthesize ideas, just as you would from the front of the room. Make notes and offer your summaries when they're appropriate.

Potential facilitator mistake: Accepting that the group doesn't want process help and letting it flounder. While it's always best to be able to "officially" facilitate, it's possible to help a group by covertly playing the process role. Some attention to process is better than none.

Scenario #2: Early in the meeting it appears the original agenda is wrong

In spite of data gathering and planning, it becomes clear that the entire premise for the meeting is wrong. The group legitimately needs to discuss something else.

Strategy: Stop the meeting and verify your assessment that the existing agenda is now redundant. Take time to do agenda building. Ask members what they want to achieve at this session. Prioritize the issues and assign times. Take a short break to regroup and create a new process design. Ratify the new agenda with the members. Be flexible and stay focused on the needs of the group.

Potential facilitator mistake: Force the group to follow the original agenda because of the energy and preparation that went into creating the design.

Scenario #3: The meeting goes hopelessly off track

Members are usually good at staying focused but have now gone totally off track and refuse to return to the planned agenda.

Strategy: Stop the off-topic discussion and determine whether members are aware that they're off topic and if they're comfortable with this. If they decide they want to stay with this new topic, help them structure their discussion. Ask:
> "How long do you want to devote to this? What's the goal of this new discussion? What tools or methods should we use?" etc.

Facilitate the new discussion. If members decide to return to the original agenda, "park" the current discussion and return to it at the end of the meeting.

Potential facilitator mistake: Stepping down from the facilitator role because the group isn't following the planned agenda or allowing the group to have a lengthy off-topic discussion without deliberately deciding that this is what they want to do. Trying to force a group back on topic when members feel a pressing need to discuss something else creates unnecessary conflict.

Scenario #4: Group members ignore the process they originally agreed on

There's a clear process for the session, but the members simply ignore it. When you attempt to get people to follow the agreed-upon method, they revert to random discussion.

Strategy: Let them go on this way for a while, then ask: *"How's this going? Are we getting anywhere?"* Once a group has recognized that it isn't making progress, members are often ready to accept a more structured approach.

Potential facilitator mistake: Give up and stop watching for an opening to step back in and offer structure. Take an "I told you so" attitude if members admit frustration with their approach.

Scenario #5: The group ignores its own norms

Members have set clear behavioral norms, but start acting in ways that break these rules.

Strategy: Allow them to be dysfunctional for a while, then ask:
"How do you feel this meeting is going in terms of the rules you set?"
"Which rules are being broken and why?"
"What can you do to adhere to these rules?"

Implement member suggestions. If they don't suggest anything, recommend that one or two group members be in charge of calling the group's attention to the rules any time they're being ignored or broken. This puts the onus on members to police themselves.

Potential facilitator mistake: Make verbal interventions without using the power of peer pressure to manage behavior.

Scenario #6: People use the session to unload emotional baggage

The agenda is swept off the table as people start venting their frustrations about their job, other people or the organization.

Strategy: Often groups can't focus on the task at hand because of pent-up feelings. In these cases, it's healthy to encourage participants to express their views. The key is to structure this venting so that it can be managed, and feelings can be channeled into actions. Useful venting questions include:
"How important is it that you share these feelings now?"
"Do we need to have any rules about how we do this?"
"How long should this go on?"

Potential facilitator mistake: Trying to suppress the venting process or letting it happen without time limits or a plan that leads to action steps.

Scenario #7: No matter what techniques are used, no decision is reached

The group has been discussing options for hours and no clear decision is emerging. The discussion is spinning in circles and precious time is being wasted.

Strategy: Stop the action and look at the decision method that's being used. There are many decisions that simply can't be made through consensus or voting. Consider using another method like using a decision grid that allows for a more objective rating of individual aspects of competing options.

Another approach is to analyze the blocks to making a final decision by asking the group to identify what's keeping them from making a decision. Record the barriers and spend time removing the key ones.

Potential facilitator mistake: Letting the group spin around for the entire meeting without checking the decision method and/or examining the decision barriers.

Scenario #8: Members refuse to report back their discussions

After a small group discussion, no one is willing to come forward and present the subgroup's ideas back to the larger group. There's a real concern that one or several of the ideas are too sensitive and that there might be repercussions.

Strategies: Divide the presentation and have two to three members from each group share the spotlight. If there's a lot of material, the whole team can present portions back to the larger group. Also set the stage with the larger group by asking them to listen with an open mind and not react negatively to the presentation before having explored its potential.

Potential facilitator mistake: Taking the burden from the members and speaking for them. This shifts responsibility for the recommendations from members to yourself, and can result in members taking little responsibility for follow-up actions.

Scenario #9: Members balk at assuming any responsibility for action plans

People love discussing problems and brainstorming ideas, but when it comes to action planning, everyone is suddenly too busy or unsure about his or her ability to complete the task.

Strategy: Make it clear from the start that any problem-solving exercise includes action planning and that members will be expected to assume major responsibility for implementing their ideas.

Implementing action plans is often a growth activity if people can be given support and encouragement to stretch beyond their present capabilities. When people are concerned that they can't succeed, help them identify what materials, training or other support they need in order to move forward.

If members have time barriers to participating in implementation, these need to be identified and problem solved. Organizations often ask the same hard-working people to be on every committee. If there's any control over who is going to be asked to work on an activity, considerable thought should be given to whether these individuals have the time needed to devote to the activity.

Potential facilitator mistake: Letting people "off the hook" too easily by not problem solving the blocks or letting the same people shoulder all of the work. The worst strategy of all is to take responsibility for the action steps yourself.

The Collaborative Conflict Management Process

The steps in managing differences of opinion collaboratively are essentially the same ones outlined in detail on pages 99 to 103 in the chapter on decision making. Once the emotions surrounding the situation have been vented, managing conflict collaboratively involves:

Step #1: ***Clarify the issue***—create a clear statement of what the issue is. Insure that everyone agrees with that statement.

Step #2: ***Identify the desired outcome***—help the members create a goal statement that describes what the situation would look like if the issue were resolved.

Step #3: ***Set a time frame***—set time limits for each step in the process.

Step #4: ***Make sure appropriate norms are in place***—if things are likely to get emotional, make sure the team has conflict norms in place.

Step #5: ***Explain the collaborative/consensual process to be used***—emphasize the need to analyze objectively before jumping to solutions.

Step #6: ***Analyze the facts of the situation***—make sure everyone is heard and that there's an objective exploration of the current situation.

Step #7: ***Generate a range of possible solutions***—use participative techniques like brainstorming or anonymous brainstorming.

Step #8: ***Evaluate the solutions***—establish objective criteria for finding the best solution and use a decision grid.

Step #9: ***Plan to implement the agreed to solutions***—make sure that the what, how, who and when are specified. Troubleshoot the action plan to make sure the steps are doable.

Interpersonal Conflict Worksheet

Behaviors that help	Person "A"	Person "B"
1. Leaning forward—listening actively		
2. Paraphrasing—"Is this what you're saying?"		
3. Questioning to clarify—"Let me understand this better."		
4. Showing respect to the other's opinion—valuing input		
5. Calmness—voice tone low, relaxed body posture		
6. Open and vulnerable—showing flexibility		
7. Clearly stating my position—assertive stance		
8. Checking for agreement on what is to be resolved		
9. Laying out ground rules—"What will help us?"		
10. Showing empathy—checking perceptions		
11. "I" statements—disclosing feelings		
12. Using other person's name		
13. Body contact—if appropriate		
14. Problem solving—looking at alternatives		
15. Win/win attitude—concern for other person		
16. Congruence—between verbal and non-verbal behavior		
17. Concern for other person's goal		
18. Feedback—giving specific descriptive details		

Behaviors that hinder	Person "A"	Person "B"
1. Interrupting		
2. Showing disrespect		
3. Entrapment questions		
4. Talking too much		
5. Pushing for solution		
6. Arguing about personal perception		
7. Aggressive manner		
8. Accusing, laying blame		
9. Smirking, getting personal		
10. "You made me" statements		
11. Non-receptive to suggestions		
12. Not identifying real feelings		
13. Ending before finishing		
14. Incongruity of words and actions		
15. Defensiveness		
16. Denying, not owning problems		
17. Blocking, talking off-topic—changing the subject		
18. Not giving specific feedback		

Use this sheet when you wish to provide detailed feedback to two people interacting during conflict.

Group Conflict Checklist

Throughout today's meeting pay special attention to the following ineffective behaviors:

No plan or process for approaching the task Group wanders from one topic to another because there's no format for discussion. No time is taken at the start of the meeting to establish a process.
Lack of active listening Instead of acknowledging each other's points before making their own, people push their own ideas without acknowledging each other.
Personal attacks People use a sarcastic tone, ignore each other, interrupt or even attack each other. They don't focus on the facts.
Lack of process checking The group forges ahead without ever stopping to assess whether the process is working or requires modification.
Dominant members A few people do all the talking. No one notices or even cares that some people are left out.
Poor time management Time isn't budgeted or monitored. Time is wasted on the wrong things.
Folding People just give in when things get rough. They don't systematically follow issues through.
Lack of skill There's no evidence that members possess decision-making tools. They also lack basic interpersonal skills.
Passive or nonexistent facilitation No one is providing order or policing the action. No notes are kept. Everyone is taking sides. If there's a facilitator, he or she is unwilling to offer procedural options or keep order.
Lack of closure The group moves from one topic to another without summarizing or identifying a course of action.

Conflict Observation Sheet

At today's meeting observe the facilitator's approach to conflict. Make note of as many specific incidents as possible to enrich the feedback.

Use this observation checklist while observing a facilitator handle conflict.

Behaviors That Help	Behaviors That Hinder
___ letting people vent	___ arguing
___ asking for dissenting views	___ defensiveness
___ paraphrasing a lot	___ asking entrapping questions
___ showing respect for opposing views	___ letting a few people dominate
___ eye contact	___ favoring one side of any debate
___ effective body language	___ letting it get emotional or personal
___ calmness	___ ending before resolution
___ non-defensiveness	___ sidestepping the really hot issues
___ validating speakers	___ not using a process
___ redirecting sarcasm	___ not using the norms
___ confronting the facts	___ lack of empathy for member feelings
___ taking a problem-solving approach	___ letting it drag on
___ using norms for control	
___ showing concern for others' feelings	
___ making interventions	
___ checking on how people are doing	
___ disclosing personal feelings	
___ ensuring a good decision is made	
___ bringing proper closure	
___ mediating conflicts between two people	
___ making sure everyone stays involved	
___ evaluating how the team did during the conflict to learn from mistakes	

Conflict Effectiveness Survey

Read over the following statements and rate how your group currently manages conflict. Be totally honest. Remember that this survey is anonymous. The results will be tabulated and fed back to the group for assessment.

Implement this survey to raise awareness of current patterns.

1. Listening

| 1 | 2 | 3 | 4 | 5 |

People assume they're right — People are open to hearing new ideas

2. Acknowledging

| 1 | 2 | 3 | 4 | 5 |

People make points without acknowledging the points made by others — People acknowledge each other's points even when they don't agree with them

3. Objectivity

| 1 | 2 | 3 | 4 | 5 |

We tend to get emotional and argue for our favorite ideas — We tend to stay calm and look objectively at the facts

4. Building

| 1 | 2 | 3 | 4 | 5 |

We tend not to admit that anyone else's ideas are good — We generally take the ideas of fellow members and try to build on them

5. Norms

| 1 | 2 | 3 | 4 | 5 |

We don't have or use norms to manage conflict situations — We have created a good set of norms that work well to help us manage conflicts

6. Trust and Openness

| 1 | 2 | 3 | 4 | 5 |

People don't say what's really on their minds — There is a lot of trust that you can say whatever you have on your mind

7. Approach to Conflict

| 1 | 2 | 3 | 4 | 5 |

Most often we either avoid or argue vehemently — We tend to collaborate to find solutions we can all live with

✎ **Conflict Effectiveness Survey, cont'd**

8. Interpersonal Behaviors

1	2	3	4	5

People often get emotional
and make personal attacks

We stay calm and stick to
the facts. No one ever
gets personally attacked

9. Structure

1	2	3	4	5

We never take a systematic approach.
Mostly we just speak our minds

There is always a clearly defined
process for discussions

10. Closure

1	2	3	4	5

Most of our conflict sessions
end without resolution

We are excellent at getting
to solutions and clear action steps

11. Process Checking

1	2	3	4	5

Once an argument starts
we never call time-out and
correct ourselves

We always stop to look
at how we're managing
our conflicts so we
can improve

12. Time Management

1	2	3	4	5

When things get heated, we
lose all track of time and our
agenda goes out the window

We carefully monitor
time to make sure
we aren't wasting it

13. Aftermath

1	2	3	4	5

People are usually angry
for a long time afterward

We work at clearing
the air of hurt feelings

Use the survey feedback process to deal with the results.

Chapter 7
Meeting Management

 ne of the key facilitator roles is to know how to design and manage effective meetings. First, sensitize yourself to the ingredients of an ineffective meeting:

 — lack of clarity about the meeting goal
- a vague or nonexistent agenda
- no time limits on discussions
- no discernible process for working on important issues
- no one facilitating discussions
- people haven't done their homework
- discussions that go off track or spin in circles
- lack of closure to discussions before moving on
- people vehemently arguing points of view rather than debating ideas
- a few people dominating while others sit passively
- meetings that end without detailed action plans for agreed next steps
- absence of any process checking of the meeting as it unfolds
- no evaluation at the end

Meetings are ineffective for a wide range of reasons.

Meetings That Work

By contrast, here are the ingredients shared by all effective meetings:

 — a detailed agenda that spells out what will be discussed, the goal of the discussion, who is bringing that item forward and an estimate of how long each item will take
- clear process notes that describe the tools and techniques that will be used
- assigned roles such as facilitator, chairperson, minute taker and timekeeper
- a set of group norms created by the members and posted in the meeting room
- clarity about decision-making options to be used
- effective member behaviors
- periodic process checks
- clear conflict-management strategies
- a process that creates true closure
- detailed and clear minutes
- specific follow-up plans
- a post-meeting evaluation

Our Meetings Are Terrible!

Below are some of the symptoms of dysfunctional meetings and prescriptions for their cure. These are, of course, easier to identify than to fix, but if you can help team members become aware of their patterns, they can begin to resolve them.

Know the signs and symptoms of ineffective meetings.

SYMPTOMS	CURES
As each person finishes speaking, the next person starts a new topic. There is no building on ideas, thus no continuity of discussion.	Have each person acknowledge the comments of the last speaker. Make it a rule to finish a point before moving forward.
People argue their views, trying to convince others that they're right rather than understanding either the issue or anyone else's input. There is no listening.	Train members to paraphrase what is said in response to their point. Use the flip chart to record all sides of an issue. Get everyone to understand these differing views.
As soon as a problem is mentioned, someone announces that he or she understands the problem. A solution is very quickly proposed and the discussion moves to another topic.	Use a systematic approach to bring structure to discussions. Become thorough in solving problems. Avoid jumping to obvious solutions.
Whenever someone disagrees with a group decision, the dissenting view is ignored.	Develop an ear for dissenting views and make sure they are heard. Have someone else paraphrase the dissenting opinion.
The group uses brainstorming and voting to make most decisions.	Pre-plan meeting processes so other tools are on hand, and then use them.
Conversations often go nowhere for extended periods. In frustration the group moves on to a new topic without closure.	Set time limits on each discussion and periodically evaluate how it's going. Use summaries to achieve closure.
People often speak in an emotional tone of voice. Sometimes they even say things to others that are quite personal.	Have people stop and rephrase their comments so there are no distracting personal innuendoes.
People use side-chats to share their thoughts.	Encourage honesty by valuing all input. Draw side-chatterers back to group conversation.
Group members don't notice they've become sidetracked on an issue until they've been off topic for quite awhile.	Call "time-out" or have some other signal to flag off-track conversations. Decide if you want to digress or park the particular issue.
The extroverts, or those with power, do most of the talking. Some people say little at most meetings.	Use round robins to get input. Call on members by name. Use idea slips to get written comments from everyone.
No one pays attention to body language or notices that some people have tuned out or even seem agitated.	Make perception checks and ask people to express their feelings.
There is no closure to most topics. Little action takes place between meetings.	Stress closure. Reach a clear decision and record it. Have an action planning form handy. Bring actions forward at the next meeting.
There is no after meeting evaluation. People debrief in their offices.	Do a meeting evaluation and discuss the results before the next meeting. Post any new rules or improvement ideas.

The Fundamentals of Meeting Management

1. Create and use a detailed agenda

Each meeting must have an agenda that's been developed ahead of time and ratified by the members of the team. By having the agenda in advance of the meeting, members can do their homework and come prepared to make decisions.

Agendas should include:

    __ the name of each topic, its purpose and expected outcome

    __ time guidelines for each agenda item

    __ the name of the person bringing each item forward

    __ the details of the process to be used for each discussion

If the agenda can't be designed in advance for whatever reason, then the first order of business at the meeting should be agenda building. In this facilitated discussion, members design the agenda for that day's session.

2. Develop step-by-step process notes

Most of the books that have been written on meetings do not mention "process notes," largely because these books are geared toward meetings that will be chaired rather than facilitated.

When a meeting is facilitated, there *must* be detailed process notes for each agenda item. These notes specify how the discussion will be facilitated. They specify the tools to be used and how participation will be managed.

In the following sample agenda, we've added process notes to illustrate their important role. While some facilitators keep these design notes to themselves, it's often a good idea to openly share the process notes with the group. (Examples of detailed process notes can be found in Chapter 9.)

Sample agenda with process notes

Name of group: Customer Fulfillment Team
Members: Jane, Muhammed, Jacques, Elaine, Carl, Fred, Diane, Joe
Meeting details: Monday, June 12, 2005, 11:00 to 1:00 (Brown Bag Lunch),
                  Conference Room C

What & Why*	How (process notes)
Warm-up (10 min) → Joe → create focus	• Members share one recent customer contact story
Review agenda and norms (5 min) → Joe → To set context	• Ratify the agenda and the norms through general discussion. Add any new items; make sure there is clarity about the overall goal of the meeting
Bring forward action items (25 min) → all members → Implementation monitoring	• Brief report back by all members on action plans created at the last meeting; addition of any new plans

A clear agenda circulated in advance is a key ingredient to success.

Facilitators always develop detailed process notes for each discussion.

What & Why*	How (process notes)
Focus group updates (20 min) ➟ Jacques & Diane ➟ To identify areas for improvement	• Report on the outcomes of six customer focus groups. Use force-field analysis to distinguish between what we are doing well and what we aren't
Prioritization of customer issues (20 min) ➟ Joe ➟ To set priorities	• Establish criteria to evaluate customer concerns • Use criteria matrix to appraise each issue and identify priorities for action
Problem solving of priority issues (30 min) ➟ entire group ➟ To create improvement plans	• Divide into two sub-teams to problem solve the two top-priority issues; create detailed action plans for the top issues; meet as a group to share and ratify ideas
Next-step planning & agenda building (10 min) ➟ Joe ➟ To insure closure & design next session	• Make sure people know what they're expected to work on; create agenda for next meeting
Exit survey (10 min) ➟ Joe ➟ To check meeting effectiveness	• Have people evaluate the meeting on their way out the door • Identify items to be brought forward at the next meeting

*Note: *Times given above are totally speculative and are only included for illustration purposes.*

Clarifying roles helps reduce overlaps and power struggles.

3. Clarify roles and responsibilities

Effective meetings require people to play defined roles.

Chairperson: runs the meeting according to defined rules, but also offers opinions and engages in the discussion if he or she chooses. The chairperson has traditionally not been neutral. Most often, the chairperson of any meeting is the official leader, who plays an active role as both decision maker and opinion leader.

Facilitator: designs the methodology for the meeting, manages participation, offers useful tools, helps the group determine its needs, keeps things on track and periodically checks on how things are going. A facilitator doesn't influence *what* is being discussed, but instead focuses on *how* issues are being discussed. A facilitator is a procedural expert who is there to help and support the group's effectiveness.

Minute taker: takes brief, accurate notes of what's discussed and the decisions made. Also responsible for incorporating any notes on flip charts. Most often, minute-taking responsibilities are rotated among the regular members of a work group. However, for special meetings or if resources allow, this role can be assigned to a neutral outsider.

Timekeeper: a rotating role in which someone keeps track of the time and reminds the group about milestones periodically. Not a license to be autocratic or shut down important discussions if they're running over. The use of an automatic timer will allow the timekeeper to participate in the discussion.

Scribe: a group member who volunteers to help the facilitator by recording group comments on a flip chart. Some facilitators are more comfortable asking others to make notes on the flip chart while they facilitate. This has the benefit of freeing the facilitator from the distraction of writing, but adds its own complications. The scribe may start facilitating or may not take accurate notes. Since having a scribe takes an additional person out of the discussion, it is an impractical strategy for small groups. It is a standard practice for facilitators to make their own notes. If a scribe is used, clarifying questions should always be channeled through the facilitator, instead of the scribe interacting directly with the members.

Balancing the Roles of Chairperson and Facilitator

Chairing and facilitating are two distinct meeting management roles. Each has its purpose and place.

Chairing is most useful at the start of a meeting in order to review past minutes, share information and manage a round-robin report-back by members.

Chairing traditionally relies on the use of pre-published rules of order.

Since chairs are not neutral, their major drawback is that they tend to influence decisions and concentrate power. It's not uncommon for a strong chairperson to make final decisions on important items.

A consequence of this decision mode is that the chair "owns" the outcome. There's also little emphasis on using process tools by traditional chairpersons.

Facilitating is designed to foster the full and equal participation of all members for items where their input is needed. Because facilitators are neutral, they empower members. They rely on consensus and collaboration to reach important decisions. This results in decisions for which the whole group feels it has ownership.

Facilitation creates rules from within the group, rather than imposing rules from a book. Facilitation is also associated with a rich array of tools and techniques designed to create synergy and get better ideas.

A very common role arrangement is to have a meeting leader who uses a chairperson approach to start the meeting and review the agenda, take care of the housekeeping and information-sharing portions of the session, and then switch to facilitation in order to get input on specific topics.

All good facilitators should know when and how to act as an effective chairperson. Conversely, it would be ideal if all chairpersons were also skilled facilitators,

Effective chairpersons know when to switch roles in order to facilitate.

who could switch roles whenever it's desirable to get participation and ownership.

With advance planning, these roles don't need to conflict. The key is to remember that each has its place, and to be clear about which approach is being used in which situations.

In summary:

Chair when you want to:	Facilitate when you want to:
• review past minutes and agenda items	• get participation & shift ownership
• hear members report back or exchange information	• engage people in planning, problem solving or relationship building
• remain accountable for decisions	• get members to make decisions

Always insure that norms are posted and accurately used.

4. Set clear meeting norms

Make sure that the group has clear norms for behavior and that those norms are created by the group. Help the group tailor its norms to meet the demands of particular meetings by engaging members in setting targeted norms if they are needed. (Refer to the Conflict Norms, page 114.)

5. Manage participation

Make sure that everyone is part of the discussion, that structure exists for each item, that there's effective use of decision-making tools and that closure is achieved for all items.

Facilitators are responsible for insuring that members know and exhibit effective group behaviors. If members lack group skills, facilitators need to conduct simple training exercises, such as those suggested on page 79.

6. Make periodic process checks

Process checking is a technique to use during meetings to keep things on track. This involves stopping the discussion periodically to redirect member attention to how the meeting is going. The purpose of this shift in focus is to engage members in a quick review in order to identify needed improvements.

There are basically four elements in process checking:

a. Check the purpose: Ask members whether they're still clear about the focus of the meeting, to make sure everyone is still on the same page.

When to check the purpose: If the conversation seems to be stuck, or if people seem to be confused; at least once per session.

b. Check the process: Ask members if the tool or approach being used is working or needs to be changed. Ask for or offer suggestions for another approach.

When to check the process: When the process tool being used isn't yielding results, or it's evident that the process isn't being followed as originally designed.

c. Check the pace: Ask whether things are moving too quickly or too slowly. Implement suggestions for improving the pace.

When to check the pace: When things seem to be dragging or moving too fast; any time people look frustrated; at least once per session/meeting.

d. Take the pulse: Ask members how they're feeling: Are they energized? Tired? Do they feel satisfied or frustrated? Ask for their suggestions about how to change energy levels.

When to take the pulse: Any time members look distracted, frustrated or tired; at least once during each session.

Using a written process check

Although process checks are usually done verbally, they can also be conducted in the form of a survey posted on a flip chart. Members are invited to anonymously rate how the meeting is going, usually as they leave the room for a break. When members return, they are asked to interpret the survey results and brainstorm ideas for improving the remainder of the session. All practical suggestions are implemented.

Regularly check the process.

Sample Process Check Survey

Tell us how it's going so far.

Purpose: *To what extent are you clear about our goals?*

1	2	3	4	5
Poor	Fair	Satisfactory	Good	Excellent

Progress: *To what extent are we achieving our goals?*

1	2	3	4	5
Poor	Fair	Satisfactory	Good	Excellent

Pace: *How does the pace feel?*

1	2	3	4	5
Far too slow	Slow	Just right	Fast	Far too fast

Pulse: *How are you feeling about the session?*

1	2	3	4	5
Totally frustrated	Exhausted	Satisfied	Pleased	Energized

---

7. Determine next steps

Never let a group leave a meeting without clear next steps in place. This means defining what will be done, by whom and when. These action plans need to be brought forward at all subsequent meetings to make sure that the group is following through on commitments.

8. Evaluate the meeting

Effective groups make it a habit of routinely evaluating meeting effectiveness. There are three basic ways to evaluate a meeting:

Meetings need to end with true closure.

1. Conduct a Force-Field Analysis – this involves asking:

"What were the strengths of today's meeting?" **(+)**

"What were the weaknesses?" **(–)**

"What should we do to correct the weaknesses?" **(Rx)**

2. Post an Exit Survey—three to four questions are written on a sheet of flip chart paper and posted near an exit. Members fill it out upon leaving the meeting. The results are brought forward and discussed at the start of the next meeting. On the next page you'll find a sample of exit survey elements.

3. Implement a Formal Survey—create a survey and distribute it to members to complete anonymously. After tabulation, the results are discussed at a subsequent meeting. This is an appropriate exercise to be done three or four times a year for any ongoing group or team. A sample formal Meeting Effectiveness Survey is provided on page 144. The Survey Feedback process is described on page 170 in Chapter Eight of this book.

Sample Exit Survey Elements

Output—To what extent did we achieve what we needed to?

1	2	3	4	5
Poor	Fair	Satisfactory	Good	Excellent

Organization—How effective was the meeting structure?

1	2	3	4	5
Poor	Fair	Satisfactory	Good	Excellent

Use of time—How well did we use our time?

1	2	3	4	5
Poor	Fair	Satisfactory	Good	Excellent

Participation—How well did we do on making sure everyone was involved equally?

1	2	3	4	5
Poor	Fair	Satisfactory	Good	Excellent

Decision Making—How well-thought-out were our decisions?

1	2	3	4	5
Poor	Fair	Satisfactory	Good	Excellent

Action Plans—How clear and doable are our action plans?

1	2	3	4	5
Poor	Fair	Satisfactory	Good	Excellent

Limit exit surveys to three or four questions.

Meeting Effectiveness Survey

Rate the characteristics of your meetings by circling the appropriate number on each scale to represent your evaluation. Remain anonymous. Return the survey to your group facilitator for review at a future meeting.

1. PREPARATION

Does everyone come prepared and ready to make decisions?

1	2	3	4	5

We are often
unprepared

We are always
well prepared

2. COMMUNICATION

Are agendas circulated to all members in advance of the meeting?

1	2	3	4	5

Agendas are rarely
circulated in advance

Agendas are always
circulated in advance

3. SETTING

Is there a quiet place for the meeting, with ample space and support materials?

1	2	3	4	5

The meeting place is
not well suited

The meeting place
is excellent

4. MEETING OBJECTIVES

Are objectives and expected outcomes clearly set out for each agenda item?

1	2	3	4	5

Objectives and outcomes
are never clear

Objectives and outcomes
are always clear

5. START TIMES/END TIMES

Do meetings start/end on time?

1	2	3	4	5

Meetings hardly ever
start/end on time

Meetings always
start/end on time

6. TIME LIMITS

Are time limits set for each agenda item?

1	2	3	4	5

We do not set
time limits

Time limits are always
set for each item

7. ROLE CLARITY

Are roles such as timekeeper, scribe and facilitator clearly defined?

1	2	3	4	5

Roles are not
clarified

Roles are always
clearly defined

Implement this survey to create impetus for improving meetings.

8. PAST MEETING REVIEW

Are action items from the previous meeting(s) brought forward?

1	2	3	4	5

Items are seldom
brought forward

Previous items are
always brought forward

9. PROCESS

Is there clarity before each topic as to how that item will be managed?

1	2	3	4	5

There is rarely any
structured process

There is always a
structured process

10. INTERRUPTIONS

Are meetings being disrupted due to people leaving, pagers, phones, etc.?

1	2	3	4	5

There are constant
interruptions

We control
interruptions

11. PARTICIPATION

Are all members fully engaged and taking responsibility for follow-up?

1	2	3	4	5

People hold back and
don't take ownership

Everyone offers ideas
and takes action

12. LISTENING

Do members practice active listening?

1	2	3	4	5

We don't listen closely
to each other

Members listen
actively

13. CONFLICT MANAGEMENT

Are differences of opinion suppressed, or is conflict effectively used?

1	2	3	4	5

We tend to
argue emotionally

We debate
objectively

14. DECISION-MAKING QUALITY

Does the group generally make high quality decisions?

1	2	3	4	5

We tend to make
low quality decisions

We tend to make
high decisions

15. LEADERSHIP

Does one person make all the decisions, or is there a sharing of authority?

1	2	3	4	5

A few people make
most decisions

Decision making
is shared

Meeting Effectiveness Survey, cont'd

16. PACE

How would you rate the pace of your meetings?

1	2	3	4	5

Poor   Excellent

17. TRACKING

Do meetings stay on track and follow the agenda?

1	2	3	4	5

Meetings usually stray   Meetings usually
off track   stay on track

18. RECORD KEEPING

Are quality minutes kept and circulated?

1	2	3	4	5

No, they're not   Yes, they are

19. CONSENSUS

Do we work hard to make collaborative decisions that we can all live with?

1	2	3	4	5

We abandon consensus   We work hard
too easily   to reach consensus

20. CLOSURE

Do we effectively end topics before getting into new ones?

1	2	3	4	5

We move on without   We close each topic
closure   before moving on

21. FOLLOW-UP

Is there timely, effective follow-up to commitments made at meetings?

1	2	3	4	5

We tend not to   There is consistent
follow up   follow-up

Note: Use the survey-feedback process described in Chapter 8 to engage participants in assessing the results of the meeting effectiveness survey in order to identify meeting improvement strategies.

Facilitating Teleconferences

More meetings are happening at a distance these days, often involving people who have never met. While facilitation was created for face-to-face meetings, there are a number of key elements that can be borrowed from the facilitator tool kit to help make distance meetings more effective.

First, let's look at some of the special challenges of meetings conducted by phone:

- People can't see each other so the meetings tend to feel impersonal and disconnected
- Interaction tends to be stilted because people can't see each other, so conversations tend towards one-way information sharing
- Since people have to wait for a chance to talk, teleconferences can drag on far too long
- Sometimes people sit in silence for long stretches listening to conversations that have nothing to do with them
- It's impossible to read body language to pick up on the non-verbal clues that identify how people are feeling or whether they're fully engaged as the meeting progresses
- If differences of opinion crop up, it's very difficult to manage the conflict effectively, bring other people into the conversation or help the parties arrive at a mutually agreeable solution
- While minutes are usually sent out afterwards, there are no flip chart notes being taken during conversations to keep everyone focused and to help the conversation move forward
- Teleconference participants could be doing any number of other tasks during the session like reading, eating, working on their computers or sorting out their desks, rather than paying attention
- It's easy for people to walk in and out of a teleconference without detection by the other participants
- If materials weren't sent out ahead of time, it's impossible to hand out new information

The facilitation techniques that most improve teleconferences are many of the same ones that work in a face-to-face meeting: providing a clear purpose, describing the process, conducting a warm-up exercise, making interventions, encouraging interaction, conducting periodic process checks, paraphrasing key ideas, offering periodic summaries, ensuring that key items have closure and clear action steps. Here is how you can use these strategies to improve any phone conference.

Borrow core tools and techniques from facilitation to improve teleconferences.

Before the teleconference:

• Contact participants by phone or e-mail to seek their input to the agenda.

• Create a detailed agenda, with process notes, that identifies the various types of conversations that will be held (information sharing, planning, problem solving, relationship building).

• Identify who needs to be involved and for which segments of the call, plus the information that each player needs to prepare.

• Distribute the agenda to the participants so they can do their homework and dial in to the call at the time they'll be needed.

At the start of the teleconference:

• Conduct a roll call to establish that people are engaged and ready to proceed. If applicable, ask each person to state what they need to get out of the meeting. Record these personal goals and refer to them throughout the meeting to help keep people engaged and let them know you have them in mind.

• Create a name map on a blank sheet of paper in front of you. Beside each name, write down their stated goal for the session. As the meeting progresses, make a check mark beside people's names every time they speak. This will remind you of who is on the line and what they need to get from the session. It will also help you identify the people who need to be brought into the conversation.

• Review the agenda to clarify the overall purpose of the call, the purpose and process for individual segments and the time associated with each segment. Also be clear about who needs to be part of which conversations.

• Clarify the rules of teleconferencing. This can be a facilitated conversation, or you can propose a core set of teleconference norms that participants can amend and ratify.

Teleconferences need their own norms.

Teleconference Norms

To insure that this call is productive, we will all:

• be as clear and concise as possible
• try to engage others by asking questions and offering our opinions
• ask for clarification if it's needed
• freely express concerns and opinions
• speak up if we notice we've been silent for too long or if a particular conversation needs to wrap up
• strive to stay focused
• ask for a summary anytime we need to get refocused
• announce if we are leaving the call

During the teleconference:

- At the start of each topic, review the purpose, process and time frame for each item.
- Call on people by name, both to present and to comment on what others have said. Keep track of who is getting air time.
- Periodically make process checks to insure that things are still on track:

Teleconference Process Checking
• Is the purpose still clear?
• Is our approach working?
• Are we making progress?
• Is the pace ok? . . . too fast? . . . too slow?
• Have we lost anyone?

- To bring closure to a topic, offer a summary of the key points that were made. If it was a decision-making discussion, turn the summary into a decision statement, then conduct a roll call of each person to ask them to accept the final decision.
- Help the group create action plans for any topics that need them. Encourage people to take responsibility for follow-through.

At the end of the teleconference:

- Review the summaries for each topic and the action steps that have been identified.
- Invite each person to say whether their goal for the meeting has been achieved, or to make a statement of what they feel they got out of the meeting.
- Conduct a brief post-telecon evaluation by asking people to identify what worked, didn't work and ideas to improve future telecons. If this is impractical, create an evaluation form on-line and deploy it through e-mail.
- Share details about when and how the minutes will be shared.
- Identify any future teleconferences.
- Express thanks for everyone's participation and sign off.

Teleconferences need closure just as much as any other meeting.

✎ Notes

Chapter 8
Process Tools for Facilitators

*I*magine a carpenter trying to build a house without the proper tools. It would certainly be ineffective, if not altogether impossible! Regardless of the job, you need the right tools. Fortunately for facilitators, there is a rich set of tools available.

Since dozens of tools exist, it would be impossible to explain them all. Only the most often used tools will be highlighted in this chapter. This set represents the basic processes that every facilitator must know how and when to use.

You'll find a detailed description of each on the following pages.

- **Visioning**
- **Sequential Questioning**
- **Brainstorming**
- **Facilitative Listening**
- **Multi-Voting**
- **Gap Analysis**
- **Force-Field Analysis**
- **Root-Cause Analysis**

- **Decision Grids**
- **Troubleshooting**
- **Wandering Flip Charts**
- **Exit Surveys**
- **Survey Feedback**
- **Priority Setting**
- **Needs and Offers**
- **Systematic Problem Solving**

In addition to these tools, all facilitators should learn the techniques associated with quality improvement such as process mapping, affinity diagrams, storyboarding, SWAT analysis, histograms, scatter diagrams and critical path charts.

Know how and when to use the core process tools

Visioning

What is it? A highly participative approach to goal setting for groups of any size.

When to use it? When members need to clarify their own thoughts and then share those ideas with each other to create a shared statement of the desired future.

What's its purpose? Allows people to put forward their ideas. Makes sure everyone is involved and heard from. Creates energy. Gets people aligned. Gives people an interactive method to identify a group goal.

What's the outcome? The visioning process is very participative and energizes everyone in the room. It also creates buy-in because the group's direction is coming from the members themselves. Everyone is involved at once. All ideas are heard. This is a great way to conduct goal-setting with a group.

How to Do Visioning

Step #1. Post a series of questions that relate to the task and ask how the final outcome ought to look at a future point in time. The vision questions will always be different, of course, depending on the situation.

> ***Sample Visioning Questions for a Customer Service Improvement Team***
> Imagine that it's exactly two years from today:
> * *Describe how you now serve customers.*
> * *What specific improvements have been made?*
> * *What are people saying about the team now?*
> * *What problems has the group solved?*
> * *What specific outcomes have been achieved?*
> * *How are people behaving differently?*

Step #2: Ask each person to write down his or her own responses to the questions. Allow at least five minutes. Give more time if needed. Ask people not to speak to each other during this writing phase.

Step #3: Ask everyone to find a partner. Ideally, this is the person they know least. Allocate three to five minutes for the first partner to share his or her vision. Ask the other partner to facilitate. After three to five minutes, ask the partners to switch roles so that the second person gets to talk.

Step #4: When time is up, ask everyone to find a second partner. Repeat the process outlined in Step #3, only allow slightly less time per person. Encourage people to "steal" any good ideas they got from their last partner and incorporate these into their own vision.

Step #5: Repeat the process again with new partners. This time, limit the exchange to one to three minutes per person in order to encourage people to prioritize and share key points.

You can stop after only a few rounds or continue until everyone has spoken to everyone else.

Step #6: Ask people to return to their original seats, and then begin facilitating a discussion to pull the ideas together. You'll find that ideas have become fairly homogenized by this point.

A good way to proceed is question by question until you have gathered all the ideas. In a very large group, you can gather ideas by using the Open Space Method described in this chapter.

Sequential Questioning

What is it? An assessment exercise in the form of a series of closed-ended questions, which are posed to the whole group at the start of a workshop.

When to use it? To uncover important information about the group, their issues or activities. To test and probe in a challenging manner. To raise issues and create awareness of shared needs.

What is its purpose? Yields information, lets you test assumptions and engages people. Allows people to safely surface complex issues. Vents negative feelings and creates an obvious need to take action. Helps the facilitator anticipate the issues that might come up throughout the day. When done well, this technique creates a shared desire for change. It also acts as a group warm-up.

What's the outcome? Sequential questioning is a challenging technique that creates sparks. It raises issues and gets people talking about the barriers. It raises people's consciousness about what the important problems are. It sets the stage for problem-solving and solution development.

Since there is potential for disagreement, if you plan to use sequential questioning, you have to be prepared to make interventions and manage differing opinions.

How to Do Sequential Questioning

Step #1: Analyze the overall topic and create five to ten questions working from macro to micro issues. Build questions around issues people identified in pre-workshop interviews. Pose the questions as closed-ended questions or items to be rated on a scale. Choose someone to answer yes or no to each item. Each question should probe the situation in a challenging way so that the ensuing discussion reveals honest information that is important to the issue at hand.

Step #2: Write each question at the top of its own sheet of flip chart paper. Use the rest of the sheet to record reactions. Don't let people see the questions until you pose them. As you turn over each sheet, read the question, pause, then ask one person in the group to respond. Record that person's response.

Then, invite others to add their thoughts. Discuss people's reasons until you have recorded all comments. It's not always necessary to get agreement, but strive to create a summary statement that expresses key ideas.

While sample questions are offered on the next page, remember that these questions always need to be created to fit each particular situation.

Sample Sequential Questions

Focus on Business Improvement

Answer **yes** or **no,** then explain your response.

yes or **no** Rationale➤	The overall business environment for the next five years is going to be advantageous for our business.
yes or **no** Rationale➤	We are fully prepared to handle all the opportunities that will occur in the next five years.
yes or **no** Rationale➤	Our current business development strategy is dynamic and flexible enough to respond to constant changes in the business environment.
yes or **no** Rationale➤	Our business strategy should be developed by people at the higher levels.
yes or **no** Rationale➤	Our staff are ready and motivated to overcome barriers.
yes or **no** Rationale➤	We completely understand our customers' needs and wants.
yes or **no** Rationale➤	We have an early warning and performance measurement system that lets us track our progress and make timely corrections.
yes or **no** Rationale➤	There is a high level of harmony and cooperation that insures synergy and teamwork inside our organization.
yes or **no** Rationale➤	We have the best products on the market. We own the market in our field.
yes or **no** Rationale➤	We have a fairly flawless delivery system for getting our product to our customers.
yes or **no** Rationale➤	We often have creative business development discussions during our regular meetings. Better customer service is a topic we discuss all the time.

Brainstorming

What is it? A synergistic technique that frees people to think creatively and generate innovative ideas.

When to use it? When it's advantagious to generate a free flow of creative ideas that are not bound by the usual barriers. To get everyone involved. To create energy. To generate a wide range of solutions for a problem.

What's its purpose? Allows people to explore new ideas and challenge traditional thinking. Lets people put ideas on the table without fear of being corrected or challenged. It separates the creation of ideas from the evaluation activity.

What's the outcome? A long list of creative ideas from which to work. Since brainstorming frees people from practical considerations, it encourages them to think creatively. It's also an energizing process that helps move people to take action. Because it's highly participative, brainstorming makes everyone feel that they're an important part of the solution.

How to Do Brainstorming

Step #1: Announce that you will be using brainstorming. Review the rules:
- Let ideas flow freely
- No evaluating of ideas until later
- Build on the ideas of others
- Keep discussion moving
- There are no bad ideas
- Everyone participates
- Think in new ways; break out of old patterns

Step #2: Clarify the topic being brainstormed, then allow some quiet while people think about solutions.

Step #3: Ask members to let their ideas flow. While you can brainstorm by going round robin around the group, brainstorming is best done spontaneously with members offering ideas as they come to mind.

Step #4: Record ideas as they're generated. Do not discuss or elaborate on them. Keep it moving.

Step #5: When people have run out of ideas, generate additional ideas by asking probing questions such as:

> *"What if money were no object?"*
> *"What would our competitors wish we would do?"*
> *"What's the opposite of something already suggested?"*

Step #6: When the flow of ideas has stopped, explore each brainstormed idea in detail so that it's fully developed and clearly understood. Combine like ideas that are simply worded differently.

Step #7: Use a decision grid (page 164) or multi-voting (page 159) to sort the ideas for action planning.

Written Brainstorming

What is it? A private and individual idea generation technique in which people write down their ideas, then pass them to other group members who build on them.

When to use it? When people are reluctant to speak in front of others, or when there are outspoken members who might dominate a traditional brainstorming session. Also useful if the issue or topic is sensitive, since the initial idea generation step is anonymous and private.

What's its purpose? The anonymity of this tool provides the freedom to encourage people to express their ideas.

What's the outcome? A lot of ideas are generated in a short time. It also allows people to build on each other's ideas in an anonymous setting.

How to Do Written Brainstorming

Step #1: Clarify the topic or issue for which ideas will be generated. Explain the process to members.

Step #2: Give each person small slips of paper. Ask members to work alone as they think of ideas to resolve the issue being discussed. Allow anywhere from three to ten minutes for the idea generation step.

Step #3: Ask members to fold their idea slips and toss them onto the center of the table. (Slips should not have names on them.)

Step #4: Mix the sheets and ask each person to take back as many as he or she tossed in. If anyone pulls out his/her own slip, that person can toss it back, or exchange it with a neighbor.

Step #5: Each person now has three to five minutes to add his or her thoughts in response to the ideas on the slips picked from the pile. The slips can then be passed to a third person to generate further ideas.

Step #6: Once all ideas have been developed, ask all members to read out loud the suggestions on the slips they now hold.

Step #7: Discuss ideas and record them on the flip chart.

Step #8: Use a decision grid (page 164) or multi-voting (page 159) to sort the most effective ideas to fit the situation.

Facilitative Listening

What is it? A technique for getting people to listen to each other and really hear each other's ideas. A way of teaching people effective listening skills.

When to use it? To insure that people really understand each other in situations where there are opposing ideas and people have a history of not hearing each other's views. As a key first step in mediating a conflict.

What does it do? Allows everyone to get a fair hearing and feel understood by the "opposing side". Circumnavigates conflicts by placing people in pairs and limiting their interactions to either presenting views or listening to understand.

What's the outcome? This structured approach to listening insures that people listen to, comprehend and acknowledge the opposing views of others. Since counter-arguments are not allowed, people have an opportunity to hear each other's views. Feeling heard relieves tension and sets a positive tone for tackling issues together.

How to Do Facilitative Listening

Step #1: Announce that you will be asking participants to take part in facilitative listening. Review the following rules:

- One person will be speaking and expressing their thoughts about the subject at hand.
- The second person will be limited in how he or she may respond. It is your job to:
  - *Stay neutral* no matter how you feel about what the other person is saying. Do not express opposing views or argue back.
  - *Listen actively* by maintaining eye contact and using attentive and open body language.
  - *Ask probing questions* after each point made by the other person to get more information.
  - *Paraphrase* what the other person is saying by repeating their main ideas to gain clarity.
  - *Summarize* what the other person has said to insure that his or her ideas have been understood.

Step #2: Clarify the topic to be addressed. Then ask everyone to find a partner. It's important that people select a partner from the "opposing" group. Ask the partner pairs to spread out around the room so that they feel they have some privacy.

Step #3: Determine how much time is appropriate for the particular topic. Set a timer and have the pairs begin their conversations. Maintain time-frames and make sure that people have the chance to play both roles.

Step #4: After the first round, stop the action and ask everyone to find a second partner. Stop after the second round or repeat the process to deepen the dialogue. The facilitative listening pairs can be repeated as often as desirable.

Step #5: If you are working with two individuals, ask each to make a short presentation back to the other person, summarizing his or her new understanding of the situation. Make sure these summaries are acceptable to both parties.

Step #6: If you are working with two groups, allow the groups to caucus separately to combine the information that each person heard into a summary of the views of the "opposing" party. Have each group appoint a spokesperson to make a presentation to the other group, summarizing their understanding of the other party's views. Check the summaries to make sure they're satisfactory.

Multi-Voting

What is it? A priority ranking tool that enables a group to quickly sort through a long list of ideas.

When to use it? To sort through a large number of choices.

What's its purpose? Rapidly establishes priorities.

What's the outcome? Multi-voting is democratic and participative. Since most members will see several items they favored near the top of the priority list, multi-voting tends to result in a sense of, *"I can live with it."*

How to Do Multi-Voting

Step #1: Clarify the items being prioritized. This may be a list of barriers from a force-field analysis or a list of ideas from a brainstorming exercise. Have members discuss each item to insure everyone understands the choices.

Step #2: Identify the voting criteria so that people don't vote at cross-purposes. Make sure that everyone votes with the same criteria in mind. Many situations benefit from voting several times, applying criteria to each vote. Examples of criteria include:

- the most important items
- the lowest cost items
- the easiest items to complete
- the first items in a logical sequence
- the most innovative items
- the most significant given the strategic direction
- the most important to our customers

Step #3: Once the criteria are clear, there are various methods for conducting a multi-vote.

Voting with sticker dots
- Using peel-off file-folder dots, hand out a strip of four to seven dots to each person. Use slightly fewer dots than half the items to be sorted to force people to make choices (i.e., give out four dots to sort ten items).
- Ask members to place their stickers on their top four choices on the flip chart. Insure that no one puts more than one sticker on any one item.
- When everyone has voted, tally the dots in order to arrive at the priorities.

Distributing points
- Give each person points (usually 10 or 100) to distribute among the items to be sorted.
- Members then write their points beside the items they favor. It's wise not to allow anyone to place more than 50% of their points on any single item.
- When everyone has voted, add the scores to arrive at the priorities.

Gap Analysis

What is it? A means of identifying missing steps needed to achieve a goal.

When to use it? When a group needs to understand the gap between where they currently are and where they ultimately want to end up.

What's its purpose? Gap analysis encourages a realistic review of the present and helps identify the things that need to be done to arrive at the desired future.

What's the outcome? Gap analysis is a planning tool that creates a shared view of what needs to be done to eliminate the gap between the present state and the desired future.

How to Do Gap Analysis

Step #1: Identify the future state. Use a tool like visioning or any other approach that generates a picture of where the group wants to be at a specific time. The description of the future must be detailed. Post the information on the right-hand side of a large blank wall.

Step #2: Identify the present state. Describe the same components featured in the future state, only do so in present terms. Again, be very detailed. Post the ideas generated on the left-hand side of the wall work space.

Step #3: Ask members to work with a partner to identify the gap between the present and the future. Ask questions like:

> *"What are the gaps between the present and the future?"*
> *"What are the barriers or obstacles to achieving the future?"*

Step #4: Once partners have finished their deliberations, share ideas as a total group and post the gaps between the "present" and the "future."

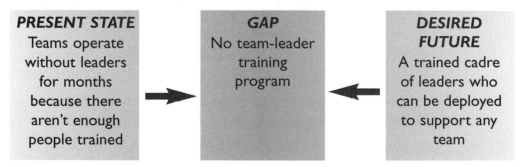

Step #5: Once there's consensus on the gaps, divide the large group into subgroups. Give each group one or more of the gap items to problem solve or action plan.

Step #6: Reassemble the whole group to hear recommendations and action plans. Ask members to ratify the plans, then create a follow-up mechanism.

Force-Field Analysis

What is it? Force-field analysis is a structured method of looking at the two opposing forces acting on a situation.

When to use it? When you need to surface all of the factors at play in a situation, so that barriers and problems can be identified. To encourage members to make a balanced assessment of a situation.

What's its purpose? Clarifies the resources available, and also the barriers or obstacles. Helps groups understand what they need to do to succeed.

What's the outcome? Force-field analysis is a valuable tool for analyzing situations and identifying problems that need to be solved. It helps groups make more effective decisions because it lets members look at both positive and negative forces at play.

How to Do Force-Field Analysis

Step #1: Identify a topic, situation or project, for example: computer training.

Step #2: Help the group state the goal of the discussion: *"All staff to receive training in the new operating system in three weeks."*

Step #3: Draw a line down the center of a flip chart sheet. Use one side to identify all of the forces (resources, skills, attitudes) that will help reach the goal. On the other side, identify all the forces that could hinder reaching the goal (barriers, problems, deficiencies, etc.).

Goal Statement: *"All staff to receive training in the new operating system in three weeks."*	
Forces that help us **Resources in place** ⟶	**Forces that hinder us** **Problems and deficiencies** ⟵
• staff eager for improved software • state of the art software • computer literate staff • four great training rooms • 80% of staff at a central location • six qualified instructors	• disruptions to work schedules • software complexity • high need for ongoing coaching • lacking at least six training rooms • 20% of staff geographically scattered • costly external instructors • bad time of year for training

Step #4: Once all the help and hinder elements have been identified, use multi-voting or a decision matrix to determine which of the hindrances or barriers are a priority for immediate problem solving.

Step #5: Address the priority barriers using the *Systematic Problem-Solving Model* (page 174).

Variations of Force-Field Analysis

Force-field analysis has a number of variations. Each is used in approximately the same way as previously described.

These variations include:

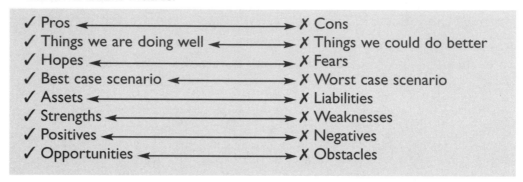

✓ Pros ⟷ ✗ Cons
✓ Things we are doing well ⟷ ✗ Things we could do better
✓ Hopes ⟷ ✗ Fears
✓ Best case scenario ⟷ ✗ Worst case scenario
✓ Assets ⟷ ✗ Liabilities
✓ Strengths ⟷ ✗ Weaknesses
✓ Positives ⟷ ✗ Negatives
✓ Opportunities ⟷ ✗ Obstacles

Root-Cause Analysis

What is it? A systematic analysis of an issue to identify the root causes rather than the symptoms.

When to use it? When you need to delve below surface symptoms and uncover the underlying causes of problems.

What's its purpose? Leads to more complete and final solutions.

What's the outcome? Root-cause analysis enables groups to look more deeply at problems and to deal with the underlying causes. This often means that problems are more likely to be definitively resolved.

How to Do Root-Cause Analysis

Step #1: Explain the difference between "causes" and their "effects" to group members. For example, you can ask whether a noisy muffler is a cause or an effect. Once people have identified that it's an effect, ask them to list all of the causes. Point out that effects can't be solved, but underlying causes can.

Step #2: Use either of the two basic methods for identifying root causes: Cause & Effect Charting or Fishbone Diagrams.

Cause and Effect Charting

i) To use this method, divide a flip chart sheet in half and write causes on the left side and effects on the right. Example: Noisy Muffler.

Causes	*Effects*
• corrosion	• noise and fumes coming from the muffler when accelerating
• loose clamps	
• puncture	

ii) Whenever anyone offers a point of analysis, ask whether it's a cause or effect. Write each item in its appropriate column. Probe each effect by asking "why" to determine what causes it. Continue until all causes have been identified.

Fishbone Diagrams

Use a fishbone diagram to sort all of the contributing causes for the situation being analyzed. The cause categories on fishbone charts vary, but usually include people, machinery/equipment, methods, materials, policies, environment and measurement. The number of categories will vary by subject.

i) Start by placing the observed effect at the "head" of the fishbone. Determine the major cause categories, then ask members to brainstorm all of the possible causes on each "rib" of the fish. For example:

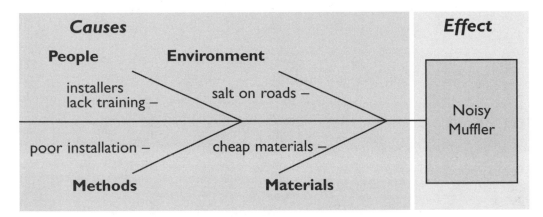

Step #3: Once all of the causes have been identified, use multi-voting to identify which causes are the highest priority for resolution.

Decision Grids

What is it? A matrix that uses criteria to assess a set of ideas in order to determine which ones are most likely to be effective.

When to use it? When you need to bring more objectivity and thoroughness to the decision-making process.

What's its purpose? To provide a structured decision-making process for dealing with a complex issue involving various elements. Transform a random debate into one in which solutions are judged against an objective set of criteria.

What's the outcome? Clear, sorted ideas emerge from a mass of random inputs. Grids also make the sorting process more systematic. Since everyone gets to cast votes or express opinions, the use of grids is participative and objective.

How to Use Decision Grids

Two types of decision grids are illustrated: *criteria-based* and *impact-effort based*.

Impact/Effort Grids

Step #1: Recreate the chart shown below on a sheet of flip-chart paper.

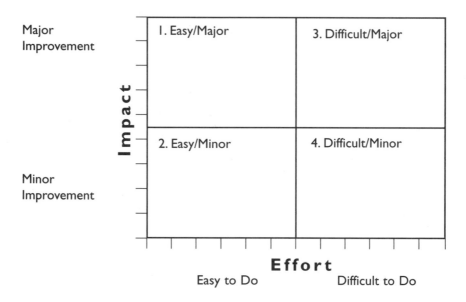

Step #2: Discuss the various choices, then place each in one of the four boxes:

1. Easy to do and yielding a big improvement
   ↳ for immediate implementation
2. Easy to do but yielding a small improvement
   ↳ for immediate implementation
3. Difficult to do and yielding a big improvement
   ↳ action as major projects
4. Difficult to do and yielding small improvement
   ↳ discarded

Impact/effort grids are easier to use than criteria-based grids because the grid has already been designed and there's no need to create criteria.

The major difficulty in using an impact/effort grid lies in clarifying exactly what is meant by the terms "easy to do," "difficult to do," "small improvement" and "big improvement," since everyone will understand these terms differently. Being clear about terminology at the start will avoid much heated debate.

Criteria-Based Grids

Step #1: Ask members to identify the criteria against which potential solutions will be judged. Examples are:

- saves time
- saves money
- reduces stress
- is timely
- is feasible
- is affordable

- supports the strategic plan
- is something we can control
- represents the right sequence
- doesn't disrupt our operation
- will get management support
- satisfies customer needs

Step #2: The relevant criteria are chosen from this list and placed along the top of a grid. The options being considered are placed down the left column. Note that some criteria may be more important than others, and hence given more weight. An example of weighted criteria uses the following scale:

(x 1) = does not meet the criteria
(x 2) = somewhat meets the criteria
(x 3) = good at meeting the criteria

Step #3: The choices are then evaluated as to the extent each meets the criteria. Scores are tallied to identify the best choice.

Decision grid for assessing solutions to the challenge of getting 50 people trained in new software in 14 days.

Criteria		Cost Effective (x 1)	Meets Customer Needs (x 3)	Speed (x 1)	Lack of Disruption (x 1)	Totals per Solution
Choices	Shut down to give all staff two days' classroom training	1 2 1 1 ÷ 4 = 1.25	1 1 1 1 ÷ 4 = 1.00	3 3 3 3 ÷ 4 = 3.00	1 1 1 1 ÷ 4 = 1.00	**8.25**
	Have experts on site for two weeks to give one-to-one support	2 2 2 1 ÷ 4 = 1.75	2 3 2 2 ÷ 4 = 2.25	1 2 1 1 ÷ 4 = 1.25	3 3 3 3 ÷ 4 = 3.00	**12.75**
	Have only 10 people off for two days at a time	2 2 3 3 ÷ 4 = 2.50	2 3 3 2 ÷ 4 = 2.50	2 2 2 2 ÷ 4 = 2.00	2 2 2 3 ÷ 4 = 2.25	**14.25**

Troubleshooting

What is it? A process for identifying potential blocks and barriers so that plans can be formulated to overcome them.

When to use it? When it's important to identify barriers to success and create action plans to deal with them. When the group has a history of poor follow-through on actions.

What's its purpose? Helps insure that action plans are well thought out. To improve the likelihood of follow-through.

What's the outcome? Groups are less likely to be "surprised" by hidden circumstances, and hence, gain more control over their work.

How to Do Troubleshooting

Step #1: After a group has created action plans, ask members to consider a series of questions. These questions force a critical look at the circumstances that might impede the activity. For example:

> *"What are the difficult, complex or sensitive aspects of our action plan?"*
> *"What shifts in the environment, like a change of priorities, should we keep our eye on?"*
> *"What organizational blocks or barriers could we encounter?"*
> *"What technical or materials-related problems could stop or delay us?"*
> *"What human resource issues should we anticipate?"*
> *"In what ways might members of this team not fulfill their commitments?"*

Step #2: Once potential barriers have been identified, ask members to identify strategies and action plans to overcome each one.

Step #3: Help the group write up its troubleshooting plans. Identify who will monitor follow-through. The following worksheet will help you lead this discussion.

Troubleshooting Worksheet

What could go wrong, block us or change suddenly?	*What actions will overcome each block?* *(what, how, by whom, when)*

Wandering Flip Charts

What is it? A safe and participative means of engaging a large number of people in productive conversations about specific issues. A way of gaining a lot of input from a large group in a short time.

When to use it? When you want to explore a wide range of topics with a large number of people and have little time to do it. To energize a group and get everyone into the conversation. When there is a topic that people may not want to talk about in open conversation. When a large open space with useable walls is available and you have a group of at least 20 people.

What does it do? Creates a relatively safe and anonymous setting for conversation. Provides an alternative means of generating group synergy since people get to read and then build on each other's ideas.

What's the outcome? A large number of issues are explored. Group ideas are developed. Everyone gets to participate and have their ideas added into the mix.

How to Use Wandering Flip Charts

Step #1: Set up the room by posting blank sheets of flip chart paper or poster paper in separate stations around the room.

Step #2: Clarify the topic or series of topics to be discussed. Then divide the topic into segments or sub-topics.

Step #3: Post one topic segment or sub-topic at the top of its own flip chart sheet.

Step #4: Instruct people to wander the room and gather at a flip chart that features a topic about which they have knowledge. Be clear that there must always be no fewer than three and no more than five people at each flip chart. Once there, the participants discuss the topic and record their collective thoughts for a specified period, typically in the range of five minutes.

Step #5: At the end of five minutes invite everyone to wander to another flip chart station, read what the first group has written and confer with whomever else wandered there in order to add more comments to the sheet. This process can be repeated until all of the flip chart sheets are filled. It is not necessary that each person visit each station.

Wandering flip chart variations and applications:

In planning exercises, the flipchart topics can coincide with various key questions in the planning process, such as: what are the key consumer trends, what competitive forces do we face, what are our manufacturing strengths, what are our manufacturing weaknesses, what are the next technological innovations we need to prepare to adopt and so forth.

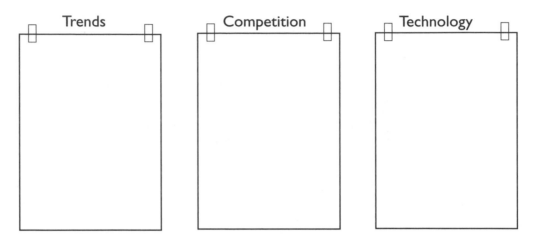

In a problem solving exercise, solve a large number of problems by posting each in a different area and then having participants wander to first analyze each problem. When all of the problems have been analyzed by at least three sets of wandering visitors, have people retrace their steps to read the completed analysis sheets and then begin to brainstorm solutions. After everyone has wandered to at least three stations to add solutions, give everyone a colored marker and invite the participants to tour all of the sheets of brainstormed solutions to check off the three ideas they think should be implemented.

Inadequate Phone System   **Lack of Volunteers**

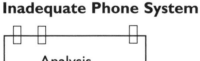
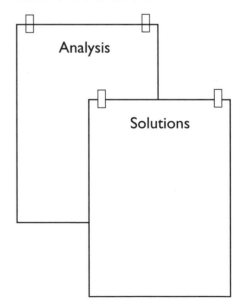

Exit Surveys

What is it? An anonymous survey that takes the pulse of the group in order to determine how things are going.

When to use it? At the end of a meeting or at a mid-point. Whenever you want to take the pulse of the group and uncover hidden feelings.

What does it do? Provides data about the effectiveness of interaction so that issues can be surfaced and addressed. Allows for venting concerns.

What's the outcome? An exit surveys acts as a "safety valve" for releasing anxieties or concerns. It channels these concerns into solutions and thus empowers the group to resolve its own issues.

How to Use Exit Surveys

Step 1: Identify two to four questions. Write these on a single flipchart sheet. The following are typical examples of exit survey questions:

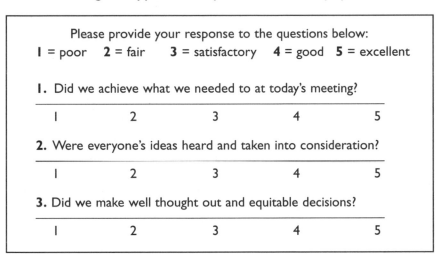

```
        Please provide your response to the questions below:
    1 = poor    2 = fair    3 = satisfactory    4 = good    5 = excellent

    1.  Did we achieve what we needed to at today's meeting?
        _____
        1           2           3           4           5

    2.  Were everyone's ideas heard and taken into consideration?
        _____
        1           2           3           4           5

    3.  Did we make well thought out and equitable decisions?
        _____
        1           2           3           4           5
```

Step 2: Post the survey sheet on a wall near the exit so group members can mark it as they exit the room. If people seem reticent, place the survey on a flipchart stand and turn it against the wall to further protect the anonymity of raters. Provide markers and ask people to make their assessments.

Step 3: At the start of the next session with that group, present the exit survey sheet. Use the survey feedback process to assess the data. This consists of the following format. For each question discuss:

> *"Why did this item receive this rating?"*
> *"What can be done to improve this rating?"*

Step 4: At the end of the discussion, review improvement ideas. These will fall into two categories: action steps or new norms. The new norms should be added to the existing norms for this team. Conduct exit surveys periodically as a preventative means of keeping meetings running effectively.

Survey Feedback

What is it? A process that involves gathering information and feeding it back to members so that they can interpret the data and identify action steps.

When to use it? When there's a problem that group members need to address, about which they lack information. As a catalyst for change.

What's its purpose? It gives the group a means of assessing how it's doing and provides a method for creating actions to resolve any identified problems.

What's the outcome? Creates a sense of commitment and accountability amongst members for making improvements.

How to Do Survey Feedback

Step #1: Design and conduct a survey. This can take an anonymous form or be an open process, such as an exit survey. The survey can be about:
- meeting effectiveness
- team/group effectiveness
- leader performance
- process effectiveness
- customer satisfaction

Step #2: After the surveys have been completed, they are returned to a designated member of the group. This person tabulates the survey results by combining all of the responses onto a blank survey form. The person doing the tabulation doesn't interpret the results; he or she just combines the ratings from the individual surveys.

Step #3: Tabulated survey results are fed back to the group. After members have had an opportunity to read the results, pose two questions:

1. *"What is the survey data telling us is going well? Which items received high ratings? Why did these items receive high ratings?"*

2. *"What is the survey data telling us are problems or issues? Which items received low ratings? Why did these items receive low ratings?"**

* A rating is considered high if 80% of respondents rated the item as either good or excellent. In the example below, nine out of 14 ratings were scored equal to or below satisfactory, which means that the feedback for this item shows cause for concern.

poor		satisfactory		excellent
1	2	3	4	5
✗✗	✗✗✗	✗✗✗✗	✗✗✗	✗✗

Step #4: Once members have identified the items that received sufficiently low ratings to be of concern, have them rank these in terms of priority to determine which should be addressed.

Step #5: Once the top priorities are clear, divide the members into subgroups of no fewer than four individuals. Give each subgroup one issue to work on for 20 to 30 minutes. Deal with as many issues as group size allows.

In subgroups, members will answer two sets of questions about the item they have been given:

1. *"Why did this item get a low rating? What's wrong here? What is the nature of the problem?"* (group members analyze the problem)
2. *"What are possible solutions for this problem? What will remedy the situation?"* (group members generate solutions)

Step #6: Reassemble the total group and ask subgroups to share their recommendations. Encourage everyone to add their ideas and to ratify their final actions. Select the best ideas and implement them.

Step #7: Ask members to briefly return to their subgroups to complete any action plans that might be needed to insure that improvements are implemented.

Priority Setting

What is it? A process for involving the members of a team or department in identifying priorities in any cutback situation.

When to use it? When there's a desire to involve the members of the group rather than having management determine the priorities.

What's its purpose? To benefit from the input and ideas of all staff. Helps members clarify their priorities and take responsibility for managing in a constrained environment.

What's the outcome? A set of priorities created by group members, which they're prepared to accept and to which they have a high level of commitment.

How to Do Priority Setting

Step #1: Identify the parameters of the priority-setting exercise. Is it to reduce budgets by 20 percent? Is it to reduce the number of products or services offered from dozens to three or four? Is it to simplify an operation? Also clarify the timelines and other realities.

Step #2: Identify all of the items that will be the focus of the priority-setting exercise. These could range from products and services to publications and office locations. If there are implications for job loss or job reassignment, these issues must be discussed openly at the start of the exercise.

Step #3: Work together to create a list of criteria for assessing the relative importance of these items. These priority-setting criteria should be created by the group to fit the specific situation. Five to seven criteria usually will suffice.

Examples include:

- Meets customer needs/expectations
- Supports the strategic direction
- Expands the business
- Creates economic benefits
- Creates social benefits
- Creates environmental benefits
- Raises our profile
- Represents a major innovation
- Is doable/feasible
- Has a positive cost/benefit ratio
- Has positive impact on staff
- Contributes to program balance

Once the criteria have been identified, construct a grid with the items to be prioritized down the left-hand column and the criteria across the top. Rate each item using a scale that reflects the extent to which it meets the criteria.

Example: **1** = low priority, **2** = medium priority, and **3** = high priority.

Example: Budget cuts at the county zoo

	Meets Needs of Public	Supports Strategic Direction	Creates Economic Benefits	Positive Cost/Benefit Ratio	Total Rating
Children's petting zoo	3	3	3	2.5	11.5
Guided tours	2	1	2	1	6
Guest speakers	1.75	2.5	1	1	6.25
Zoo magazine for kids	2.5	3	2	1	8.5

Step #4: Before individuals rate each item, openly discuss each item in detail. Since the final decision is made through individual ranking, this total group discussion is essential. It's especially important if jobs are at stake. In some priority-setting exercises, it may be advantageous to add "weight" to the criteria. For details on weighted criteria, see page 165, in this chapter.

Step #5: Individuals then rank the items according to their understanding of how well each item meets the criteria.

Step #6: Scores are added, then divided by the number of raters, and results discussed. Discussion questions include:

"Did the right priorities emerge?"

"What are the scores telling us?"

Step #7: Refer the results of the priority-setting exercise to the body responsible for translating the priorities into actual budget numbers. The final cutback plan should be shared with the whole group to keep the process open and participative.

Needs and Offers

What is it? A constructive dialogue between two parties to identify action steps they can take to improve the relationship. A positive and constructive dialogue that lets people express past and present concerns about the relationship in totally constructive terms.

When to use it? To encourage dialogue between parties to either resolve a conflict or improve relations proactively before problems occur.

What's its purpose? To vent concerns and resolve interpersonal issues in a low risk manner. To negotiate a new, more positive relationship.

What's the outcome? An improved understanding of each other's views and feelings. Mutually agree to action plans that will enhance relations.

How to Do Needs and Offers

Step #1: Clarify who will be the focus of the exercise. This can be a team and its leader, two subgroups of the same team, a team and management, or two individuals.

Step #2: Set a positive climate for the exercise by talking about the value of giving and receiving feedback. Make sure that the appropriate norms are in place to encourage members to speak freely and honestly.

Step #3: Explain the rules of the exercise. The two parties will be separated for a period of twenty to thirty minutes. During that time, each party will identify what they need from the other party in order to be effective.

This process is identical if the parties are two individuals or a team and its leader.

Step #4: When each party has written its "needs list," bring them back together to share their thoughts, one at a time. While one party is sharing their needs, the other must listen actively, then provide a summary of the other party's needs.

Step #5: Once parties have heard and acknowledged each other's needs, separate them again for twenty or thirty minutes while they consider what they're prepared to offer to the other party.

Step #6: Bring the parties back together and have them take turns sharing their offers. Allow for discussions of clarification. End the conversation by having members ratify what they have heard and make commitments to follow through.

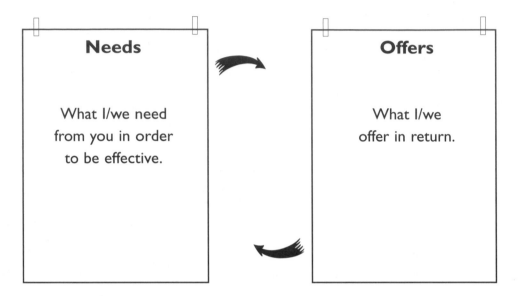

Systematic Problem Solving

What is it? A step-by-step approach for resolving a problem or issue.

When to use it? When members need to work together to resolve a problem.

What's its purpose? Provides a structured and disciplined means for groups to explore and resolve an issue together. In-depth analysis insures that groups understand their problem before jumping to solutions. This is probably the most fundamental and important facilitator tool.

What's the outcome? Systematic problem solving results in doable action steps that members of the group take responsibility for implementing. Because the process is systematic, it discourages members from randomly suggesting ideas. Problem solving is at the heart of collaborative conflict resolution. It's also a key activity in any organization that is dedicated to improving customer service and continuous process improvement.

How to Do Systematic Problem Solving

Step #1: Name the problem. Identify a problem that needs to be solved. Analyze it briefly to insure that there's a common understanding of the issue. Then support the group in writing a one- or two-sentence description of the problem. This is called the problem statement.

Step #2: Identify the goal of the problem-solving exercise. Ask the group questions such as: *"If this problem were totally solved, how would you describe the ideal situation"* or *"How will things look if we solve this problem?"* Summarize this in a one- to two-sentence goal statement.

Step #3: Analyze the problem. If the problem is fairly technical, do a detailed analysis using a *Fishbone Diagram* (see page 163). Otherwise, ask a series of probing questions to help members think analytically about the problem. Categorize the observations as either "causes" or "effects." The goal is to get to underlying root causes of the problem.

Some useful questions during analysis could include:

- Describe this problem to me in detail, step by step.
- What is it? How does it manifest itself?
- What are the noticeable signs of it?
- What makes this happen?
- How are people affected?
- What other problems does it cause?
- What are the most damaging aspects?
- What stops us from solving it?
- Who gets in the way of solving it?
- What are the root causes of each symptom?

Step #4: Identify potential solutions. Use *Brainstorming* (page 155) or *Written Brainstorming* (page 156) to generate potential solutions. When the ideas stop flowing, ask probing questions to encourage members to dig deeper. Some useful probing questions include:

- What if money were no object?
- What if you owned this company?
- What would the customer suggest?
- What if we did the opposite of the ideas suggested so far?
- What is the most innovative thing we could do?

Step #5: Evaluate solutions. Use Multi-Voting, a Criteria-Based Decision Grid or an Impact//Effort Grid to sift through the brainstormed ideas to determine which are most applicable to the situation.

Step #6: Create an action plan. Identify the specific steps needed to implement the chosen solutions. Specify how things will be done, when and by whom.

Each action step should also feature performance indicators that answer the question, "*How will we know we have been successful?*" This will help focus the action step and make it easier to measure results.

Step #7: Troubleshoot the plan. Use the troubleshooting worksheet to identify all of the things that could get in the way and then insure that there are plans in place to deal with them.

Step #8: Monitor and evaluate. Identify how the action plans will be monitored and when and how the results will be reported on. Create and use a monitoring and report-back format.

Note: Systematic problem solving is a collaborative decision-making process that builds consensus. It is parallel to the steps of consensus building described on pages 99–103 in Chapter Five about decision making.

Systematic Problem Solving Worksheet #1

Step 1. Name the problem

Identify the problem that needs to be solved. Analyze it in just enough detail to create a common understanding. Use the space below to explore the general nature of the problem.

Now narrow in and select the specific aspect you wish to solve. Write a one- or two-sentence problem statement to define the problem clearly.

Problem statement:

_____

_____

_____

_____

Systematic Problem Solving Worksheet #2

Step 2. Identify the goal of the problem-solving exercise

Describe the desired outcome. Ask:

"What would things look like if the problem disappeared?"
"How would things look if this problem were resolved?"

Use the space below to record the ideas generated.

Now narrow in and write a one- or two-sentence goal statement.

Goal statement:

_____

_____

Systematic Problem Solving Worksheet #3

Step 3. Analyze the problem

Dissect the problem thoroughly. Avoid coming up with solutions. Instead, concentrate on making sure that everyone is clear about the specific nature of the situation. Don't focus on symptoms, but delve behind each effect to determine the root causes.

Use a Fishbone Diagram if the problem is a complex technical issue that has many contributing factors. If it isn't a mechanical problem, use Cause and Effect Charting by asking questions such as:

"How would we describe this problem to an outsider?"

"What is taking place? What are the signs and symptoms?"

"How are people affected? What makes this happen?"

"What are the root causes of each symptom?"

"What other problems does it cause?"

"What are the most damaging aspects?"

"What and who stops us from solving it?"

*"How do **we** contribute to the problem?"*

Systematic Problem Solving Worksheet #4

Step 4. Identify potential solutions

Use Brainstorming or Anonymous Brainstorming to generate a range of potential solutions to the problem.

When brainstorming, remember the rules:

> • let ideas flow: be creative, don't judge
> • all ideas are good, even if they're way-out
> • build on the ideas of others

Probing questions to ask once the initial flow of ideas has stopped:

"What if money were no object?"

"What if I owned this company?"

"What would the customer suggest?"

"What's the opposite of something already suggested?"

"What is the most innovative thing we could do?"

Record brainstormed ideas here:

Systematic Problem Solving Worksheet #5

Step 5. Evaluate the solutions

Use the Multi-Voting, a Criteria-Based Decision Grid or the Impact/Effort Grid shown below to sort through the brainstormed ideas and identify a course of action.

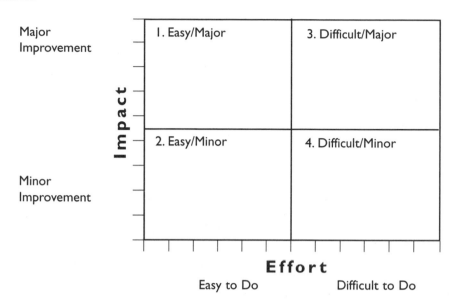

List all of the type 1 & 2 activities together for quick action	List all of the type 3 activities here for development into action plans

Systematic Problem Solving Worksheet #6

Step 6. Plan for action

Create detailed action plans for items to be implemented. Insure that action plans adhere to a logical sequence of steps. Provide details about what will be done, how and by whom. Always include target dates for completion. Identify the performance indicator that answers the question: *"How will we know we did a good job?"*

What will be done & how?	By whom?	When?	Performance Indicator

Systematic Problem Solving Worksheet #7

Step 7. Troubleshoot the action plan

Identify the things that could get in the way of successful implementation of the action plan. Create anticipatory strategies to deal with each blockage.

Use the following questions to help identify trouble spots:

"What are the most difficult, complex or sensitive aspects of our plan?"
"What sudden shifts could take place to change priorities or otherwise change the environment?"
"What organizational blocks and barriers could we run into?"
"What technical or materials-related problems could stop or delay us?"
"Should we be aware of any human resources issues? Which ones?"
"In which ways might members of this team not fulfill their commitments?"

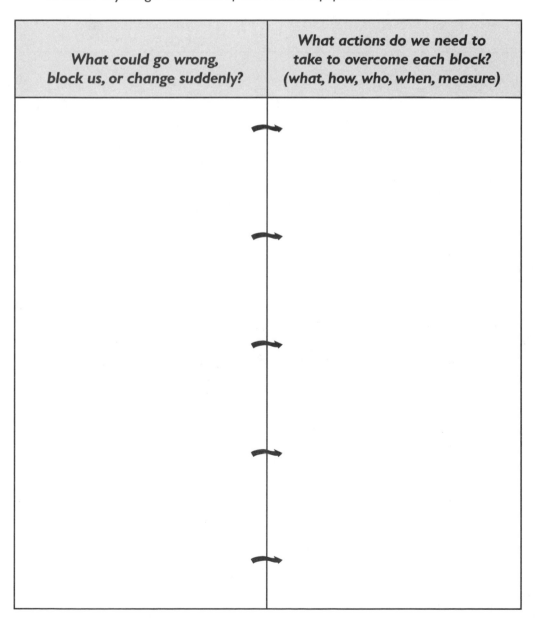

What could go wrong, block us, or change suddenly?	**What actions do we need to take to overcome each block? (what, how, who, when, measure)**

Systematic Problem Solving Worksheet #8

Step 8. Monitor and evaluate

To insure that action plans are actually implemented, identify:

How will progress be reported?   Written _____ Verbal_____

When and how often will reports be made? _____

Who needs to be advised?_____

How will results be monitored? _____

Will there be a final report?_____

Who will take responsibility for the above actions? _____

_____

_____

Reporting on Results

What activities have been implemented?	What results have been achieved?
Remaining items	**Expected dates for completion**

Chapter 9
Process Designs

*J*ust as an architect wouldn't dream of showing up at a construction site without a well-thought-out design, facilitators need to create detailed blueprints for each session.

In fact, one of the most important skills of a facilitator is the ability to create meeting designs that address specific needs. Having the right process design is just as important to the success of any meeting as being able to manage the interpersonal dynamics.

On the following pages you'll find sample process designs. These illustrate the flow of specific types of meetings and show how individual tools and techniques might be used together. Since these times and sequences are *totally speculative*, it's unlikely that any of these samples will fit real-life situations well enough to be applied straight from the book. In fact, no design should ever be borrowed from somewhere else. Part of the challenge of facilitation is creating the right design to fit the situation.

Most designs are created through a rigorous process, which includes:
- conducting background research (for example, reading reports and making site visits)
- interviewing and/or surveying members to identify specific goals and needs
- creating a preliminary design
- obtaining ratification of the design by a few or all members
- writing an agenda with detailed process notes
- communicating the agenda in advance of the meeting
- preparing needed worksheets, handouts and overheads
- designing an appropriate evaluation form

Whether you're a full-time facilitator or not, it's important to remember that professional facilitators charge as much time for research and design as they do for actually facilitating a session. This is to encourage you to spend as much time preparing as you do facilitating.

Facilitators create custom designs to fit specific situations.

Introduction to the Sample Agendas

The sample agendas on the following pages are offered as an illustration of how various tools and techniques can be combined.

Each design is accompanied by a set of specifications and assumptions that explain the context for the activities chosen. All agenda items are accompanied by facilitator notes that describe the tools and techniques used. Handout materials, overheads and other props are not included in this section, although you can find many elsewhere in this book. At the conclusion of this chapter is a Session Planning Worksheet to assist you with planning your next session.

Sample Process Designs	Page
1. Creating a mission statement and objectives	186
2. Work planning, roles and responsibilities	188
3. Priority setting/cutback planning	189
4. Inter-group negotiation	191
5. Finding and solving problems	193
6. Core program development	194
7. Survey feedback/Issue census	197
8. New leader integration	198
9. Transition planning	200
10. Process improvement	202

Sample Design #1 — Creating a Mission Statement and Objectives

Specifications: This is a new team coming together for the first time to create a clear, common goal and specific, measurable objectives. The eight members are passing acquaintances. Three hours have been set aside for this discussion.

Agenda	Process Design Notes
Welcome and agenda overview (5 minutes)	• Review the purpose of this meeting and how the three hours will be spent
Introductions (25 minutes)	• Each person chooses a partner to interview; ask name, job, skills, family info, hobbies or interest, hopes and fears about being on this team • Partners present each other to the group • Record hopes and fears
Mission statement (60 minutes)	• Present the original rationale behind the team's formation and any other available parameters • Ask members to work *alone* to answer key questions:

Agenda	Process Design Notes
	What products and services are we responsible for? *What is our unique contribution that will help the organization achieve its goals?* *What must be noteworthy about our products and services?* *In summary, what is our mission?* • After members have written their responses, have each person sit with a partner and share his/her thoughts. • After two minutes per person, have everyone find a new partner with whom to share ideas. • After two rounds, share ideas with the whole group. Synthesize ideas together. • Create a one- or two-sentence mission statement. • Post the statement on the wall.
Team Norms (10 minutes)	• Ask members: *What sorts of behaviors will make it a pleasure to be on the team? What rules should the team impose on itself to make sure that we build a positive team climate conducive to effective teamwork?* • Facilitate to pull together ideas from everyone. • Record ideas on flip chart and post on wall.
Team Objectives (80 minutes)	• Divide members into pairs, and ask them to identify, without going into great detail, what the team needs to do to achieve the team's mission. • Have members share their lists with the whole group to insure there is agreement about activities. • Provide input about how to create detailed objectives. • Ask members to work alone to write an objective for each of the identified activities. • Review and fine-tune the objectives; make sure they have been recorded for distribution.
Exit Survey	• Give members a short survey to complete before they leave. Questions can include: On a scale of 1 to 5, rate: *How well-informed do you now feel about the team?* *How comfortable are you with the mission?* *How appropriate and realistic are the objectives?*
Adjourn	• Clarify the time, place and agenda of the next meeting.

Sample Design #2—Work Planning, Roles and Responsibilities

Specifications: This is a new team that has met once to create a mission statement and objectives, but has not started to work together in closely linked roles. Three hours have been set aside for this discussion. There are eight members.

Agenda	Process Design Notes
Welcome and agenda overview (5 minutes)	• Review the purpose of this meeting and how the three hours will be spent.
Review exit survey from last meeting (20 minutes)	• Post the tabulated exit survey results. • Divide the large group in half and let the sub-groups talk for five minutes on each of the questions. *What are the issues raised by the results?* and *What can we do to remedy each of the issues?* • Reassemble as a large group and share ideas for improving the team; plan for action; record ideas.
Work planning (90 minutes)	• Make sure everyone has a copy of the team's objectives. Clear up any questions. Insure members have information about items, such as budgets, at their fingertips when planning. • Ask members to identify the characteristics of a good work plan (for example, well balanced, allows people to try new skills, etc.). • For each objective, ask people to identify what needs to be done, how and when. Allow time for individual work. • Ask individuals to write each objective and related work activities on flip chart sheets. One objective per sheet. Post sheets around the room. • Hold a discussion of each item so that members can comment, share ideas, make changes.
Roles and responsibilities (60 minutes)	• For each objective and related activities, ask members to identify the time, skills and other requirements of each activity. • Rank activities as high, medium or low, based on the degree of complexity, difficulty and time required for each. • Begin matching people with activities. Start by allowing each person to select his or her top item. Keep assigning tasks until all items are accounted for. Use the criteria to insure that no one person has all the difficult tasks, while someone else has all the simple and low time demand tasks. • Check the work plan against the criteria set at the start; ratify it and then post.
Adjourn	• Clarify the time, place and agenda of the next meeting.

Sample Design #3—Priority Setting/Cutback Planning

Specifications: This meeting is being held in response to a management directive to cut 20 percent from the budget. Some programs have to go to make the needed cuts. The members have worked together for years in the same department. There are 18 members, plus a manager. A three-hour discussion is planned.

Agenda	Process Design Notes
Welcome by director (10 minutes)	• Information sharing about the purpose of the session. Encourages staff to accept the current challenge. Offers guidelines for the cutback exercise. Sets a positive tone. Q & A.
Agenda overview (5 minutes)	• Facilitator reviews the activities of the session. (director leaves)

Hopes, fears and norms (20 minutes)	• Facilitator asks members to choose a partner. Partners interview each other:
	   Hopes: What's the best outcome we could hope for?
	   Fears: What's the worst thing that could happen?
	   Norms: What rules or guidelines do we need to impose on ourselves to make this exercise work?
	• Have members share ideas and record outcome. Make sure there is a consensus on the norms. Post on a wall.

Activity review (45 minutes)	• On a large, empty wall, hang several sheets of flip chart paper and draw a decision matrix chart. • Ask members to list each activity, program or service currently being offered. • Share information about each activity so that everyone understands its purpose, customers, costs, benefits, difficulty, time demands and any other vital factors. It's a good idea to have people prepare these activity profiles ahead of time to save time at the session. • Write the activities that will be subjected to cutbacks in the left column of the decision grid.
Establish criteria (20 minutes)	• Divide the members into subgroups of three or four members. Have the subgroups identify the criteria that ought to be used to rate the activities. Refer to the process tool section of this book for examples of criteria. • Facilitate a discussion to agree on the set of criteria to be used. Use multi-voting to sort the top five criteria if too many are initially proposed.

Sample Design #3 (cont'd)

Agenda	Process Design Notes
Rate the activities (20 minutes)	• Write the final criteria along the top of the decision grid. Clarify if any of the criteria should be given a greater significance than any others. Apply weights of 1x, 2x, or 3x to each criteria. • Explain the voting process. Let people work out their ratings on their own in their seats. When they're done, invite people to come up to the wall and record their ratings for each program.
Discuss the ratings (30 minutes)	• Once everyone has rated the activities, add all of the scores to arrive at totals for each activity. • Ask members: *What do the ratings tell us are our priority activities, programs and services? Do we agree? Are there things we should consider eliminating or at least trimming back? Do we agree?*
Propose action steps (30 minutes)	• Subdivide the members into twos and threes. Assign them each one or more of the lower-rated activities. Ask people to discuss what sorts of alterations can and should be made to that program or service to help achieve the 20 percent reduction. • Reassemble the large group to share cutback ideas and get further input from the rest of the group. • Help the group make decisions and come to closure.
Adjourn	• Insure that there are clear next steps in place. Help members identify the time, place and purpose of their next meeting.

Special Note: *In many priority-setting sessions, the participative portion of the activity ends here. Management or a small subgroup takes the information from the ranking exercise and makes the final cutback decisions. This is often a wise course of action, as it may be unfair to ask people to suggest elimination of their own jobs or roles.*

Sample Design #4 — Inter-Group Negotiation

Specifications: This is a session with two teams who recently became embroiled in a dispute. They may be fighting over equipment, staff, customers or budgets. The team leaders have tried to settle this, but the members continue to battle on. There are eight people on each team for a total of sixteen members, including the two team leaders. There are four hours for this intervention.

Agenda	Process Design Notes
Welcome, agenda overview (15 minutes)	• Information is shared about the purpose of the session and how it came about. Team leaders speak to the members about the need to cooperate and approach this with a collaborative mind-set. The details of each step in the negotiation are discussed.
Introductions (30 minutes)	• Create pairs, with one person from each team; ask people to interview each other to get information such as name, job or role, special interests or hobbies and anything else that's relevant. • Members present their partners to the whole group.
Team presentations (20 minutes)	• Give teams 10 minutes each to do a brief presentation about the team: what they do, their customers, their successes, etc.

Hopes, fears, norms (30 minutes)	• Everyone finds a new partner on the other team to discuss:
	   Hopes: *What's the best outcome we could hope for today?*
	   Fears: *What's the worst thing that could happen today?*
	   Norms: *How should we conduct ourselves today to insure that relations don't worsen?*
	• Have members share ideas and record the outcomes. Ask challenging questions and make suggestions to insure that a complete set of norms is developed.

Perception sharing (40 minutes)	• Briefly explain the rules and language of giving feedback to insure that everyone is clear on how feedback is different from criticism. • Give teams twenty minutes or so to create a point-form description of the current situation. They can describe exactly what happened, when and what the impacts of those actions were. • Separate the group, preferably in different rooms, while they talk to construct their sides of the story. Have each team choose a spokesperson to present its side. • Reunite the two teams and explain that while one group talks, the other team members can't interrupt or use negative body language. They must listen to what the other team is saying even if they disagree totally. They can, however, ask clarifying questions.

Sample Design #4 (cont'd)

Agenda	Process Design Notes
Perception sharing, cont'd (40 minutes)	• Ask one side to tell the other their perception of what is causing tensions. When the team is finished, the spokesperson from the other team offers a summary of what's been said, paraphrasing only his or her understanding, not agreeing or disagreeing. This step is purely a listening/understanding exercise. • Repeat the process with the second team.

Needs and offers (30 minutes)	• Once each team indicates that the other team has accurately understood what each has presented, the teams are separated again.
	• Each team chooses a facilitator to discuss the following two items on which they will report back to the rest of the group:
	    "What do we need from the other team to resolve this situation?"
	    "What are we prepared to do to resolve the situation?"
	• The teams return to the large room and take turns presenting their wants and offers to each other. Again, the spokesperson for the listening team paraphrases what was said to make sure there are no misunderstandings.

Action planning (40 minutes)	• Once everyone has heard the wants and offers of the other team, the facilitator leads a discussion to negotiate final actions and help members create doable action plans that will help resolve the tensions. • Finalize the action plans and make sure there is a time and date set to meet with team spokespersons to follow up.
Adjourn	Insure that there are clear next steps in place. Help members identify the time, place and purpose of their next meeting.

Sample Design #5 — Finding and Solving Problems

Specifications: This meeting is being held to identify and solve recurring problems being experienced by a department. The 20 members have been working together for some time. There are three hours for this activity.

Agenda	Process Design Notes
Welcome and agenda overview (5 minutes)	• Review the purpose of the meeting and how the three hours will be spent. • Review the group's norms. • Clarify any parameters or limits, like spending ceilings, that may impact the problem-solving activity. Also clarify the empowerment of members to solve this problem.
Clarify the focus (5 minutes)	• Have someone briefly describe the program, service or activity that is being explored. Make sure everyone is clear on what is being discussed.

Force-field analysis (20 minutes)	• Have members draw on their experience and any data gathered before the session to respond to the force-field questions:
	    "What are we doing really well, and what should we keep doing the same way?"
	    "What aren't we doing well, and what needs to improve?"

Multi-voting (20 minutes)	• Once the problems are listed and understood by all members, create criteria for identifying which blocks should be removed first. The voting criteria could be the biggest blocks, or the easiest to remove. • Hand out peel-off dots or distribute points; let members vote. • Tally the votes to reveal the ranking of the blocks.
Problem solving (90 minutes)	• Take the top 3 or 4 blocks and subdivide the large group into subgroups to tackle one problem each. • Explain the steps in the Systematic Problem-Solving Model. Give out the worksheets. Have each subgroup appoint a facilitator. • Circulate among the groups to make sure they don't get stuck on any parts of the model.
Plenary (40 minutes)	• Bring groups together at the end to share their recommendations and action plans. Invite others in the group to add their ideas. • Have subgroups refine their plans and submit them to the minute taker. • Help the group plan its follow-up mechanism to insure there are report-backs on progress made.
Adjourn	Insure that there are clear next steps in place. Help members identify the time, place and purpose of their next meeting.

Sample Design #6 — Core Program Development

Specifications: This is a session for a long-established department or division within an organization that has lost its focus. The members now wish to review what they're doing and get back on track to achieve their main business. All of the members know each other. There are 24 people, and the session is planned to last from 8:30 a.m. to 4:30 p.m.

Agenda	Process Design Notes
Welcome and agenda overview (5 minutes)	• Review the purpose of the meeting and how the day will be managed.
Context setting (25 minutes)	• Senior manager puts the core program challenge into clear context, clarifies the empowerment of the group to make recommendations and lays out his or her hopes and fears. • Question and answer session to get clarity on any issues members may have.

Hopes, fears and norms (20 minutes)	• Facilitator asks everyone to choose a partner. Partners interview each other:
	    Hopes: "*What would be the best outcome today?*"
	    Fears: "*What's the worst thing that could happen?*"
	    Norms: "*What rules or guidelines should we impose on ourselves to overcome the potential pitfalls of a core business discussion?*"
	• Partners report back information discussed.
	• Flip chart norms for setting group parameters.

Environmental scan (30 minutes)	• In the same room, divide members into subgroups of six people. Ask each group to choose a facilitator. Have them discuss:
	    "*What is happening around us?*" (In the marketplace/community/government, etc.)
	    "*What trends will have an impact on us?*"
	• Hold a brief plenary to share ideas between the subgroups.
	• Synthesize all ideas together on a flip chart.
	• Post summary on the wall.

Customer profile (30 minutes)	• The same subgroups choose a new facilitator and discuss:
	    "*Who are our customers today?*" (describe)
	    "*Who will our customers be tomorrow?*"
	    "*Who are those customers—what do they want/need?*"
	• Hold a brief plenary to share ideas.
	• Post the customer profile.

Agenda	Process Design Notes
Current focus (30 minutes)	• Ask subgroups to create a profile in response to these question: *"What business are we currently in?"* *"What are our current products and services?"* • When the products and services list is complete, pull together a complete list and write down the left-hand column of a *Criteria-Based Decision Grid*. • Post the grid, but don't develop it further at this time.
Strengths analysis (30 minutes)	• Have members return to subgroups and choose the next facilitator to discuss: *"What are our current strengths and capabilities? What are we especially skilled at?"* • Hold a brief plenary to share ideas between groups. Post strengths analysis.
Visioning (60 minutes)	• Reassemble entire group and give each person a blank piece of paper. Allow up to ten minutes for individuals to answer the following questions without talking to another member. Imagine that today is exactly three years from now and we are hugely successful: *"What business are we in? Describe our products and services. Who are our customers? What distinguishes us from the competition? What specific results have we achieved?"* • Once individuals indicate that they have answered the questions, have everyone find a partner and proceed as per the instructions for *Visioning*. • Facilitate a plenary discussion to synthesize ideas. Insure there is clarity about the desired future of the organization. • Help members write a statement that describes what their core business needs to be. • Post the statement and key points on the wall.
Mid-point check	• Post a mid-point check survey on the wall and ask members to respond to the questions as they leave for lunch or a break. These can be about progress being made, the process, the pace, etc. • When the meeting resumes, review the ratings and make improvements.
Ranking products and services (45 minutes)	• Return to the decision grid. Down the left side add any future activities, products or services that were agreed to in the visioning exercise.

Sample Design #6 (cont'd)

Agenda	Process Design Notes

Ranking products and services, cont'd (45 minutes)	• Facilitate a discussion to establish criteria to rank the items. Potential criteria can include:
	  • Supports the core business
	  • High profitability
	  • Builds on current strengths
	  • Meets a growing customer need, etc.
	• Write the criteria along the top of the decision grid, then other items. Assign weights of 1x, 2x, and 3x.
	• Have each person do his or her own ranking. Then ask members to write their rankings on the chart.

Ranking analysis (80 minutes)	• When all rankings are tabulated, ask subgroups to hold discussions to analyze the rankings:
	  "What do the rankings tell us we should be focusing on in support of our core business?"
	  "What do we need to start doing?"
	  "What do we need to keep on doing?"
	  "What do we need to stop doing?"
	• Facilitate a plenary to synthesize ideas and reach agreement on priorities for action.
	• Categorize activities/programs/services under three headings:
	New activities that need to be developed;
	Existing activities to be trimmed;
	Existing activities to be eliminated.

Strategy development (90 minutes)	• Post the activities under the three headings and let members sort themselves according to their skills, interests and knowledge. • Have subgroups take responsibility for developing action plans that develop new opportunities, reduce activity or divest programs. The process for strategy development can center around the following questions: *"What's involved in starting/trimming/stopping this activity? List steps. Who's likely going to be affected? What are the implications? What's the likely cost/benefit? What are the next steps: what should be done, how, by whom, when and with what result?"* • Hold a plenary to share ideas and have all action plans ratified by the whole group. • Help the group members identify how and when they will monitor and report on progress.
Evaluation (20 minutes)	• Evaluate member satisfaction by asking each person to comment on his or her feelings about the day. Compare these with hopes and fears set at the start.
Adjourn	• Insure that there are clear next steps in place. Help members identify the time, place and purpose of their next meeting.

Sample Design #7 — Survey Feedback/Issue Census

Specifications: A division or department within an organization wishes to identify its issues using a survey. This can be an employee satisfaction survey, a customer satisfaction survey or a survey of the performance of a product or process. There are 36 people, who have been working together for some time, at this three-hour survey feedback meeting. The survey being discussed was conducted in the weeks preceding this meeting; results were tabulated and a copy of the final tally sheets was given, without interpretation, to all members.

Agenda	Process Design Notes
Welcome and agenda overview (5 minutes)	• Review the purpose of the session and the survey feedback method.
Review survey results (25 minutes)	• Lead the whole group through a review of each question. Discuss: *"Is this a high or low rating? Is everyone clear about what this question meant?"* • Without interpreting the results, sort the responses into three categories: Items scored as good or high; Items scored as poor or low; Borderline items.
Interpreting the results (60 minutes)	• Divide the members into subgroups of six members. • Ask each subgroup to appoint a facilitator. Give each group only one issue to work on. • Groups are to work through the following questions and steps in connection with their survey item: *"Why did these items get such low ratings?"* (analyze the situation) *"What are some actions that could improve these ratings?"* (brainstorm solutions) *"Which of our solutions do we think are most promising?"* (impact/effort grid or decision grid)
Plenary (60 minutes)	• Have members share their assessments in order to benefit from each other's comments, and ratify the solutions being proposed.
Action planning (30 minutes)	• Have members return to their original subgroups to develop action plans for ideas ratified by the larger group.
Plenary (30 minutes)	• Ask subgroups to inform the rest of the members of their specific action plans for implementing the discussed improvements. • Make sure members have a plan for monitoring, reporting and follow-up. • Evaluate the effectiveness of the session.
Adjourn	

Sample Design #8—New Leader Integration

Specifications: An established team or department, with a good track record, is about to receive a new leader. The organization is concerned that the new leader be integrated quickly. It's also hoped that the transition be smooth. The new leader integration session is conducted in stages over a period of three hours. Any number of staff can attend. The first stage takes place the week before the leader joins the group.

Agenda	Process Design Notes
Stage 1 Welcome and agenda overview (10 minutes)	• At a preliminary planning session not attended by the leader, review the purpose of the new leader integration session and explain the process.

Profile preparation
(90 minutes)
	• Ask members to prepare a profile of the group. This profile will be given to the new leader in advance of a joint session. It should include:
	    "Who are we?" (our purpose, products/services, staff/skills)
	    "What are we most proud of?"
	    "What are we doing very well at this time?"
	    "Why are we doing so well in this area?"
	    "What aren't we doing that well? Why not?"
	    "What are we doing to improve?"
	    "What's ahead for us in six months, one year, three years?"
	    "Under what leadership style do we work best? Why?"
	    "How empowered have we been/should we be? For which activities?"
	    "What do we need from our new leader?"
	    "What are we offering our new leader?"
	• The notes from this discussion should be recorded and typed for distribution.

Stage 2 Leader preparation	• The facilitator meets with the new leader and brings him/her the group profile. The leader is asked to read the profile, prepare one about him/herself along the same lines and be ready to discuss his/her leadership style and philosophy of empowerment. • The leader is asked to be ready to discuss what he/she needs from the group and what he/she's prepared to offer.
Stage 3 Welcome and agenda overview (10 minutes)	• At the meeting of the members and the new leader, review the steps of the process.
Member presentation (60 minutes)	• Members are given the opportunity of speaking first to share their profile, needs and offers.

Agenda	Process Design Notes
Member presentation, cont'd (60 minutes)	• The leader is asked to listen and ask clarifying questions only.
Leader presentation (30 minutes)	• The leader is given the opportunity of presenting his/her profile, including leadership style, wants and offers, etc. Members are asked to listen and ask questions.
Discussions and negotiations (30 minutes)	• Once both parties have heard each other, the facilitator manages a discussion of any of the points where there appear to be differences or a need for further exploration. • If any item needs an action plan, the facilitator can help the group identify its next steps.
Adjourn	• Have a coffee break planned to encourage social mixing.

Sample Design #9 — Transition Planning

Specifications: A division or a department within an organization is about to undergo major change. Some staff will trade jobs. Others will trade territories. Some people will gain new titles. Others will need to acquire new skills. This planning exercise is being conducted to insure that nothing slips between the cracks and that customer service levels remain high during the actual changeover period. Twenty-four people are involved. A full day has been set aside for the transition discussion.

Agenda	Process Design Notes
Welcome and agenda overview (5 minutes)	• Review the purpose of the meeting and how the session will be conducted.
Buy-in to the process (30 minutes)	• Have everyone find a partner to interview. Pose the following questions for partners to ask each other: *"Why is it important that we have a transition plan?"* *"Why should we be the ones to create it?"* *"What would be the best possible outcome?"* *"What would be the worst outcome?"* *"What norms or rules should we impose on ourselves today to make sure that we create a fair plan everyone can live with?"* • Facilitate a discussion to gather up major thoughts and post these.
Information sharing (45 minutes)	• Presentations by those driving the change, detailing what needs to happen and when. • Question and answer session.
Identifying challenges (45 minutes)	• Divide the members by existing work groups if applicable, or create random subgroups of three to four members. • Ask them to use *force-field analysis* to identify: *"What aspects of the change are going to be relatively easy?"* *"What aspects of the change are going to be complicated/challenging?"* • Hold a plenary to create a common force field. • Use multi-voting to rank the challenges from most to least complicated/challenging.
Strategy development (120 minutes)	• Help the whole group identify the characteristics of an effective transition. This can include things such as, "doesn't disrupt customer service," or "allows people to get on-the-job coaching," etc. • Post these criteria. • Take the top four changes that were ranked to be most challenging or complicated and post these at four places around the room. • Ask members to go to the "change challenge" that involves them so that people who will be responsible for implementing each plan are in each group.

Agenda	Process Design Notes

Strategy development, cont'd (120 minutes)	• Ask each subgroup to identify a facilitator and hold a strategy development discussion.
	• The following discussions make up this process:
	  1. Describe the old state—*What activities/products/services are involved? What skills, roles, and responsibilities are associated with each activity?*
	  2. Describe the new state—*What activities/products/services define the future state? For each activity: what are the skills, roles and responsibilities? What are the implementation dates? What is negotiable versus non-negotiable? What can go wrong?*
	  3. Transition planning—*Given the time frames, is there a logical sequence of steps for implementing the change in stages? How many hand-offs are there? How can these be handled to insure continuity? Given the new roles, who needs training/on-the-job coaching? What signals can be put in place to help us monitor the transition to insure things don't go too far off track?*

Plenary (60 minutes)	• Have subgroups share their proposed transition plans. Encourage others to offer comments to fill in any gaps in the plans. Make sure the subgroup plans are linked together to form a coherent whole. Check carefully for clarity and true consensus. Insure that sensitive change issues are discussed and brought to proper closure.
Action planning (60 minutes)	• Have subgroups fill out action planning sheets that identify what will be done, how, by whom and when. • Bring groups together one last time to hear each other's action plans. Insure that notes are available for distribution soon after the meeting.
Communications planning (30 minutes)	• Ask members to identify who needs to be given information about the transition plan. • Record the communications strategy, specifying who needs to know what and when. • Insure that clear responsibility is taken for communicating the details of the transition.
Monitoring (15 minutes)	• Help the group identify how it will monitor the plan and report on progress. • Set a date for the next meeting. • Go around the room and ask members how they felt about the day.
Adjourn	

Sample Design #10 — Process Improvement

Specifications: A work group has received information that one of its key product/services/activities is problematic. The week before the session, a subgroup meets for three hours to prepare a process map showing each step of the current process. When the map is complete, key internal stakeholders and selected external customers are interviewed to gain their perspective on how the process currently functions. Eighteen people, who know each other well, will be at the session; about three hours is available to find viable improvement ideas.

Agenda	Process Design Notes
Welcome and agenda overview (5 minutes)	• Review the purpose of the meeting and how the session will be conducted.
Buy-in and norms (15 minutes)	• Ask members to find a partner to discuss two questions: *"Why is it important to improve this particular process?"* *"What rules should we set for ourselves today to make sure we reach consensus on improvements that will really make a difference?"* • Facilitate a plenary to synthesize the ideas of the partners. • Post key ideas and norms.
Map review (45 minutes)	• Ask the members who constructed the process map to explain all of the steps they identified. • Encourage the rest of the members to ask questions and add any missing details. • Ratify that the map is acceptable to all present. • Have members who did the interviews hand out copies of the data gathered and share highlights. Encourage questioning by others.
Force-field analysis (45 minutes)	• Facilitate the whole group in a force-field analysis exercise as they identify: *"What does the data tell us is working well? What is fine as it is?"* *"What does the data tell us isn't working well? What needs improvement?"* • Use multi-voting to identify the priority issues that need to be resolved by this group at this day's session.
Problem solving (60 minutes)	• Post the top three issues in different parts of the room. • Ask members to divide themselves into groups based on interest and knowledge to work on these issues. • Review the steps of the problem-solving model and ask subgroups to select one or more facilitators to manage the session. • Hold a plenary to share recommendations and ratify action plans.
Next steps (10 minutes)	• Insure that a time and date have been set for the next meeting to follow up on the action plans. • Evaluate the session.

Session Planning Worksheet

To aid you in planning your next session, consider the following:

Purpose of the session: _____

_____

_____

Number of members: _____ Do they need to be introduced? Y / N

1. What will you do to warm up the group?

_____

_____

_____

_____

2. Do you need to develop special targeted norms for this activity? If yes, what should the norming questions be?

_____

_____

_____

3. Will buy-in be a problem? If yes, what's the buy-in question to ask?

_____

_____

_____

_____

4. What background information, empowerment parameters or other constraints do members need to know?

_____

_____

_____

_____

_____

_____

_____

5. What are the key questions that need to be answered in order to arrive at the answers the group will be seeking?

_____

_____

_____

_____

_____

_____

_____

_____

6. What activities/process tools do you expect to be using at the session?

_____
_____
_____
_____
_____
_____
_____
_____

7. What could go wrong at the session? (Possible considerations: interpersonal conflicts, cynicism, lack of energy, overwhelming task, unable to achieve closure, lack of skills, etc.) For each possible problem, also identify strategies to overcome it.

Session Barriers	Solutions

8. What evaluation questions should you plan to ask at the start?

_____
_____
_____
_____

At the mid-point check?

_____
_____
_____
_____

On the final evaluation form?

_____
_____
_____
_____

9. What audiovisual aids, videos and other props will you need?

_____
_____
_____
_____

About the Author

INGRID BENS is a consultant and trainer with a Master's Degree in Adult Education and over 25 years' experience as a facilitator.

While Ingrid now spends much of her time writing about and teaching facilitation, she has extensive experience as an Organization Development Consultant.

Over the years Ingrid has designed and led numerous strategic change initiatives. She has also consulted on many team implementation projects and helped with the implementation of a variety of projects aimed at creating more collaborative workplaces.

Ingrid Bens is an expert on Win/Win negotiations and is often asked to mediate inter-group conflicts and make sensitive interventions to help dysfunctional teams.

Ingrid Bens maintains a close relationship with a number of national and international organizations including the International Association of Facilitators, Competitive Advantage Consulting, The Graduate School at U.S.D.A., The Banff Center for Management, The University of North Texas Center for Collaborative Workplaces and Goal/QPC.

For more information about the author, her other books and her training workshops go to: www.participative-dynamics.com

Acknowledgments

I wish to thank many people who provided their wisdom and insight to this second edition. First I would like to once again thank my colleagues who contributed to the first edition. These include Marilyn Laiken, Michael Goldman, Mary House, Bev Davids, Carl Aspler and Charlotte de Heinrich.

In this second edition I wish to thank all of the students in my many facilitation skills classes who continuously made suggestions and asked for additional materials. Special thanks to those who made written contributions including Mark Vilbert, Charles Bens, James Rollo and Carol Tornatore.

Bibliography

Chapter 1

Argyris, C. (1970) *Intervention Theory and Method.* Addison-Wesley. Reading, Mass.

Beckhard, R. (1969) *Organization Development: Strategies and Models.* Addison-Wesley. Reading, Mass.

Bennis, W.G. (1966) *Changing Organizations.* McGraw-Hill. New York.

Block, P. (1999) *Flawless Consulting* (2nd ed). Jossey-Bass/Pfeiffer. San Francisco.

Block, P. (1987) *The Empowered Manager.* Jossey-Bass. San Francisco.

French, W.L., & Bell, C. H., Jr. (1978) *Organization Development.* Prentice Hall. Englewood Cliffs, N.J.

Hargrove, R. (1995) *Masterful Coaching.* Jossey-Bass/Pfeiffer. San Francisco.

Jongewood, D., & James, M. (1973) *Winning with People.* Addison-Wesley. Reading, Mass.

Kayser, T. A. (1990) *Mining Group Gold.* Serif Publishing. Segundo, Calif.

Lewin, K., & Hanson, P. *Giving Feedback: An Interpersonal Skill.* In Bennis, W.G. and others. (1976) *The Planning of Change* (3rd ed). Holt Rinehart & Winston. New York.

Lippit, G.L. (1969) *Organization Renewal.* Appleton, Century, Crofts. New York.

McKroskey, J.C.; Larson, C.E.; & Knapp, M.L. (1971) *An Introduction to Interpersonal Communication.* Prentice Hall. Englewood Cliffs, N.J.

Nadler, D.A. (1977) *Feedback and Organization Development.* Addison-Wesley. Reading, Mass.

Schein, E. H., & Bennis, W. G. (1965) *Personal and Organization Change Through Group Methods: The Laboratory Approach.* Wiley. New York.

Schein, E. H. (1969) *Process Consultation: Its Role in Organization Development.* Addison-Wesley. Reading, Mass.

Schein, E. H. (1987) *Process Consultation: Lessons for Managers and Consultants.* Addison-Wesley. Reading, Mass.

Chapter 2

Argyris, C. (1970) *Intervention Theory and Method.* Addison-Wesley. Reading, Mass.

Beckhard, R. (1969) *Organization Development: Strategies and Models.* Addison-Wesley. Reading, Mass.

Blake, R.R., & Mouton, J.S. (1968) *Corporate Excellence Through Grid Organization Development.* Gulf. Houston, Tex.

Block, P. (1999) *Flawless Consulting.* Jossey-Bass/Pfeiffer. San Francisco.

Lewin, K., & Hanson, P. *Giving Feedback: An Interpersonal Skill.* In Bennis, W.G. and others. (1976) *The Planning of Change* (3rd ed). Holt Rinehart & Winston. New York.

Likert, R. (1967) *The Human Organization.* McGraw-Hill. New York.

Lippitt, G., & Lippitt, R. (1978) *The Consulting Process in Action.* Jossey-Bass/Pfeiffer. San Francisco.

Margulies, N., & Wallace, J. (1973) *Organizational Change: Techniques and Applications.* Scott, Foresman. Glenview, Ill.

Nadler, D.A. (1977) *Feedback and Organization Development.* Addison-Wesley. Reading, Mass.

Reddy, B. (1994) *Intervention Skills: Process Consultation for Small Groups and Teams.* Jossey-Bass/Pfeiffer. San Francisco.

Schein, E.H. (1969) *Process Consultation: Its Role in Organization Development.* Addison-Wesley. Reading, Mass.

Schein, E.H. (1987) *Process Consultation: Lessons for Managers and Consultants.* Addison-Wesley. Reading, Mass.

Chapter 3

Argyris, C. (1964) *Integrating the Individual and the Organization.* Wiley. New York.

Beckhard, R., & Harris, R.T. (1969) *Organizational Transitions: Managing Complex Change.* Addison-Wesley. Reading, Mass.

Dyer, W.G. (1987) *Team Building.* Addison-Wesley. Reading, Mass.

Likert, R. (1961) *New Patterns of Management.* McGraw-Hill. New York.

McGregor, D. (1960) *The Human Side of Enterprise.* McGraw-Hill. New York.

Pfeiffer, J.W., & Jones, J.E. (1972) *A Handbook of Structured Experiences for Human Relations Training* (vols I–X). Jossey-Bass/Pfeiffer. San Francisco.

Schein, E.H. (1969) *Process Consultation.* Addison-Wesley. Reading, Mass.

Schutz, W.C. (1966) *The Interpersonal Underworld.* Science and Behavior Books. Palo Alto, Calif.

Tuckman, B.W. (1965) Development Sequences in Small Groups. *Psychological Bulletin.*

Weisbord, M.M. (1991) *Productive Workplaces.* Jossey-Bass. San Francisco.

Chapter 4

Bennis, W.G. (1966) *Changing Organizations.* McGraw-Hill. New York.

Bennis, W.G. and others. (1976) *The Planning of Change* (3rd ed). Holt Rinehart & Winston. New York.

French, W.L., & Bell, C.H., Jr. (1978) *Organization Development.* Prentice Hall. Englewood Cliffs, N.J.

Kayser, T.A. (1990) *Mining Group Gold.* Serif Publishing. Segundo, Calif.

Pfeiffer, J.W., & Jones, J.E. (1972) *A Handbook of Structured Experiences for Human Relations Training* (vol I–X). Jossey-Bass/Pfeiffer. San Francisco.

Scannell, E. E., & Newstrom, J. (1991) *Still More Games Trainers Play.* McGraw-Hill. New York.

Schein, E. H., & Bennis, W. G. (1965) *Personal and Organization Change Through Group Methods: The Laboratory Approach.* Wiley. New York.

Schein, E.H. (1969) *Process Consultation: Its Role in Organization Development.* Addison-Wesley. Reading, Mass.

Schein, E. H. (1987) *Process Consultation: Lessons for Managers and Consultants.* Addison-Wesley. Reading, Mass.

Senge, P., and others. (1994) *Fifth Discipline Fieldbook.* Doubleday. New York.

Wood, J.T., Phillips, G., & Pederson, D.J. (1986) *Group Discussion: A Practical Guide to Participation and Leadership.* Harper and Row. New York.

Chapter 5

Avery, M., Auvine, B., Streiel, B., & Weiss, L. (1981) *Building United Judgment: A Handbook for Consensus Decision Making.* The Center for Conflict Resolution. Madison, Wis.

DeBono, E. (1985) *Six Thinking Hats.* Key Porter Books. Toronto.

DeBono, E. (1993) *Serious Creativity.* HarperCollins. New York.

Fisher, A.B. (1974) *Small Group Decision Making: Communication and Group Process.* McGraw-Hill. New York.

Fisher, R., & Ury, W. (1983) *Getting to Yes.* Penguin Books. New York.

Harvey, J.B. (1988) *The Abilene Paradox and Other Meditations on Management.* Heath. Lexington, Mass.

Kuhn, T.S. (1970) *The Structure of Scientific Revolutions.* University of Chicago Press. Chicago.

Schneider, W.E. (1994) *The Reengineering Alternative: A Plan for Making Your Current Culture Work.* Irwin. Burr Ridge, Ill.

Van Gundy, A.B. (1981) *Techniques of Structured Problem Solving.* Van Nostrand Reinhold. New York.

Chapter 6

Beckhard, R. (March 1967) The Confrontation Meeting. *Harvard Business Review 45.*

Beckhard, R. (1969) *Organization Development: Strategies and Models.* Addison-Wesley. Reading, Mass.

Blake, R.R., Shepard, H., & Mouton, J.S. (1965) *Managing Intergroup Conflict in Industry.* Gulf Publishing. Houston, Tex.

Filley, A. C. (1975) *Interpersonal Conflict Resolution.* Scott, Foresman. Glenview, Ill.

Fisher, R., & Ury, W. (1983) *Getting to Yes.* Penguin Books. New York.

Kilmann, R.H., & Thomas, K.W. (1978) Four Perspectives on Conflict Management: An Attributional Framework for Organizing Descriptive and Normative Theory. *Academy of Management Review.*

Kindler, H.S. (1988) *Managing Disagreement Constructively.* Crisp Publications. Los Altos, Calif.

Likert, R., & Likert, J.G. (1976) *New Ways of Managing Conflict.* McGraw-Hill. New York.

Thomas, K.W., & Kilmann, R.H. (1974) *The Thomas Kilmann Conflict Mode Instrument.* Xicom. Tuxedo, N.Y.

Walton, R.E. (1987) *Managing Conflict: Interpersonal Dialogue and Third Party Roles.* Addison-Wesley. Reading, Mass.

Chapter 7

Bradford, L.P. (1976) *Making Meetings Work.* Jossey-Bass/Pfeiffer. San Francisco.

Doyle, M., & Straus, D. (1976) *How to Make Meetings Work: The New Interaction Method.* Berkley Publishing Group. New York.

Dyer, W.G. (1987) *Team Building.* Addison-Wesley. Reading, Mass.

Frank, M. O. (1989) *How to Run a Meeting in Half the Time.* Simon and Schuster. New York.

Haynes, M. E. (1988) *Effective Meeting Skills: A Practical Guide for More Productive Meetings.* Crisp Publications. Los Altos, Calif.

Jones, J. E. (1980) Dealing with Disruptive Individuals in Meetings: *The 1980 Annual Handbook for Group Facilitators.* Jossey-Bass/Pfeiffer. San Francisco.

Chapter 8

Beckhard, R. (1969) *Organization Development: Strategies and Models.* Addison-Wesley. Reading, Mass.

Delbecq, A.L., & Van de Ven, A. H. (1971) A Group Process Model for Problem Identification and Problem Planning. *Journal of Applied Behavioral Science.*

Deming, W. E. (1986) *Out of Crisis.* MIT Center for Advanced Engineering Study. Cambridge, Mass.

Fritz, R. (1990) *The Path of Least Resistance.*

Fritz, R. (1991) *Creating.* Fawcett Columbine. New York.

Green, T.B., & D. F. R. (1973) *Management in an Age of Rapid Technological and Social Change.* Southern Management Association Proceedings. Houston, Tex.

Ingle, S. (1982) *Quality Circle Masters Guide.* Prentice Hall. Englewood Cliffs, N.J.

Ishikawa, K. (1990) *Introduction to Quality Control.* 3A Corporation. Tokyo.

Massarik, F. (1990) *Advances in Organization Development.* Ablex Publishing Corporation. Orwood, N.J.

Ouchi, W. (1981) *Theory Z.* Addison-Wesley. Reading, Mass.

Pfieffer, J.W., & Jones, J.E. (1972) *A Handbook of Structured Experiences for Human Relations Training* (vol I–X). Jossey-Bass/Pfeiffer. San Francisco.

Senge, P., and others. (1994) *Fifth Discipline Fieldbook.* Doubleday. New York.

How to Use the Accompanying CD-ROM

System Requirements
PC with Microsoft Windows 98SE or later
Mac with Apple OS version 8.6 or later

Using the CD with Windows
To view the items located on the CD, follow these steps:

1. Insert the CD into your computer's CD-ROM drive.
2. A window appears with the following options:
   Contents: Allows you to view the files included on the CD-ROM.
   Software: Allows you to install useful software from the CD-ROM.
   Links: Displays a hyperlinked page of websites.
   Author: Displays a page with information about the Author(s).
   Help: Displays a page with information on using the CD.
   Exit: Closes the interface window.

If you do not have autorun enabled, or if the autorun window does not appear, follow these steps to access the CD:

1. Click Start -> Run.
2. In the dialog box that appears, type d:<\\>start.exe, where d is the letter of your CD-ROM drive. This brings up the autorun window described in the preceding set of steps.
3. Choose the desired option from the menu. (See Step 2 in the preceding list for a description of these options.)

Using the CD with a Mac
1. Insert the CD into your computer's CD-ROM drive.
2. The CD-ROM icon appears on your desktop; double-click the icon.
3. Double-click the Start icon.
4. A window appears with the following options:
   Contents: Allows you to view the files included on the CD-ROM.
   Software: Allows you to install useful software from the CD-ROM.
   Links: Displays a hyperlinked page of websites.
   Author: Displays a page with information about the Author(s).
   Contact Us: Displays a page with information on contacting the publisher or author.
   Help: Displays a page with information on using the CD.
   Exit: Closes the interface window.

To Download Documents
The documents on this disk are duplicated in two application formats: Microsoft Word files and a single PDF file. To download a document, first open it. For Windows users, under the File pull-down menu, choose Save As, and save the document to your hard drive. You can also click on your CD drive in Windows Explorer and select a document to copy to your hard drive.

In Case of Trouble

If you experience difficulty using the CD-ROM, please follow these steps:

1. Make sure your hardware and systems configurations conform to the systems requirements noted under "System Requirements" above.
2. Review the installation procedure for your type of hardware and operating system.

   It is possible to reinstall the software if necessary.

To speak with someone in Product Technical Support, call 800-762-2974 or 317-572-3994 M–F 8:30 A.M. – 5:00 P.M. EST. You can also get support and contact Product Technical Support at http://www.wiley.com/techsupport.

Before calling or writing, please have the following information available:

* Type of computer and operating system
* Any error messages displayed
* Complete description of the problem.

It is best if you are sitting at your computer when making the call.